THE WHOLLY BIBLE
WHAT I INTENDED

JESUS, THE CHRISTED

HeartHouse *Publishers*

DISCLAIMER

This book is designed to provide information in regard to the subject matter covered. Any application of the recommendations set forth in the following pages is at the reader's discretion and sole risk. It is sold with the understanding that the publisher, author and distributors are not responsible for any disruptive conditions which may arise emotionally, mentally, spiritually or physically as a result of this book. The reader is hereby advised that you are responsible for your own well being.

HeartHouse Publishers, PO Box 1795, North Bend, WA 98045-1795.

FIRST EDITION
PRINTED IN CANADA

Library of Congress Cataloging-in-Publication Data

Jesus, the Christed (Spirit)
    The wholly Bible: what I intended / Jesus, the Christed [channeled through I.M. Hart].—1st ed.
        p. cm.
        ISBN 0-9642866-9-6

        1. Spirit writings. 2. Jesus Christ—Spiritualistic interpretations.

Welcome Beloved,
to the Heart of
Mother–Father God.

CONTENTS

The Wholly Bible: What I Intended is the first of a series of books which are being delivered to awaken the reader to the greater truths which need to be understood if we as a race of people hope to survive our creative process. This book is about recognizing and owning our divine heritage. The truth has been obscured and many are lost to the original messages of Jesus. Everything has evolved intellectually on this planet and yet nothing has evolved spiritually or emotionally for almost 2,000 years. There is much work to be done.

ABOUT THE INDIVIDUAL WHO RECEIVED THIS BOOK

Mother–Father God and the Christ communicate with all life. I have chosen to listen. I am a simple individual, leading a simple life. I have dedicated my life to the seeking of truth, and to the preservation of all life that embraces life. I do not present this book to you as the gospel truth, nor do I profess to be Jesus. I do not seek followers because there is but one master, and that master is the Christ within your heart. I choose to remain anonymous. I do profess that I am a loving and compassionate individual with a deep desire to share that which Mother–Father God and the Christ have communicated through me. I believe that when an individual is blessed with certain truths that can enhance the overall quality of life, there arises a sense of obligation to share them with humankind. In doing this, truth is assured its position of power as the evolving presence which permeates all life.

Receiving this book has helped me to recognize my own Christedness by allowing me to see:

1) who, why, and where Mother–Father God is;
2) my denials and judgments;
3) that my heart is a reflection of Christ's Heart/ Love; and
4) that I AM a fragment of heaven manifest on earth.

As a condition of publishing this book, HeartHouse Publishers has agreed to protect my anonymity. This book is not about knowing who I am; it is about you knowing who you are. It was delivered to assist you in recognizing your own Christedness.

DEDICATED
TO
THE RESTORATION OF
THE PRESENCE OF HEART

THE WHOLLY BIBLE
WHAT I INTENDED

It is not the children who fear different religions or truths. It is the adults who are rigid and frozen with fear because they have forgotten the innocence of their own childhoods. And it is the ones who have forgotten, who pass this ignorance from generation to generation.

CHAPTER I

What I Intended

"These things that I do, so shall ye do, and even greater things shall ye do."

What I said was what I intended. You are a reflection of Mother–Father God and are no less capable than I. If you will release the illusion of your separation from Mother–Father God, you will become as one Heart—a self-realized manifestation of love. My vision of one Heart was that all nations or tribes would become a political, economical, and philosophical melting pot of shared resources. I wanted spirituality to unite all peoples and beliefs and all hearts with the truth about the one Heart. What has caused your heart to become fragmented from its parental Heart is the illusion of separation. Belief in the illusion that you are separate from Mother–Father God spawns the denials that plague the peoples of this planet. This book is about how these denials came into manifestation and how they continue to plague my original intent.

During my incarnation as Jesus my physical body was no different from that of any other human being who walked this earth. I too was cloaked in the same physical flesh as you. My parents were not Mr. and Mrs. Joseph Christ. Rather, I was Jesus who became "Christed" through the discovery of the mighty I AM presence/Heart. By my ego's acceptance of my mighty I AM presence/Heart I became the only begotten son of Mother–Father God. The word "only" means "one." Children are not born to be separate from Mother–Father God. Separation is an illusionary belief of the ego; it is not the desire of Mother–Father God or me. Mother–Father God has given all free Will choice. The original sin was and is the ego's acceptance of the illusionary belief that it was and is separate from Mother–Father God. Your beliefs create your world, and once your ego believes itself to be separate, so shall it be cut off from my presence as well as from the inheritance of my Mother and Father in heaven. It is through your ego's acceptance and remembrance of Mother–Father God's presence manifest within your Heart that you become Christed as the only begotten Daughter/Son of Mother–Father God.

4

tellect with which to understand new awareness. Your lack of acceptance for Mother God creates a lack of balance/Heart. The things you are creating are coming into manifestation without being questioned as to whether they will be good for all life.

The second most tragically popular denial is in seeing Mother–Father God as a trinity, when in reality we are a quaternary. It is not Father, Son and Holy Ghost; but rather Mother, Father, Heart/Christ and Form. What is being denied is that Mother–Father God and I can be experienced in the physical body. We are as one. We are whole. This is why I have selected the word "wholly" for use in the title of this book; it means to comprise or involve all.

The third most tragically popular denial is in the misunderstanding of the symbol of the cross. The cross was used as a symbol representing two flows of energy long before it became a symbol of my crucifixion. The vertical line represents the flow of energy connecting the spiritual realms with the physical realms. The horizontal line represents physical consciousness in its karmic desire for physical experiences. The center of the cross represents these forces in balanced harmony with one another, as does the Yin/Yang symbol. This balance is the purpose of my essence. This balance that is my Heart is also your Heart, and when you live your life with the balance of Heart, there is no separation between heaven and earth.

I want to tell you about your denied presence of Heart. What used to be a fiery glow of green light tinged with gold and pink—centered in the middle of your chest—has been reduced to a small spark polarized to your left side. Your left side represents your receptive aspect and your right side represents your giving aspect. The left side represents the feminine aspect of your personality, regardless of whether you have a female or a male form. The reason I have polarized to your left side is because your feminine side is seriously in need of love and acceptance.

You have been taught that it is better to give than to receive, but now you must learn to receive if you hope to survive. You must learn to receive your left side with the same equality as that of your right side.

Your left side is the source of your power. It is your connection with Mother–Father God and your Soul/Spirit. As such it is the source of your emotional body, your intuition, your instincts, your dreams, and the feminine aspect of your sexuality. Your right side is your power to implement. It is your connection with the physical dimension and your ego. As such it is the source of your mental body, your intelligence, and the masculine aspect of your sexuality. In order to balance the left and right aspects of your being, you must go through Heart. Heart represents love/acceptance—both for yourself and for the Divine.

Many have been waiting for me to return, and yet my return can only happen when there is a willingness to receive me unconditionally through the Christing of each individual. Revelations is not meant to occur at some distant date. It is meant to be happening always. **"The time is fulfilled, and the kingdom of Mother–Father God is at hand. Forgive and receive, and believe in this truth."**

8

My hope is to prepare you for the coming spiritual changes which are necessary if life, as you now know it, is to continue. Everything has evolved intellectually on this planet, and yet nothing has evolved spiritually or emotionally for over 2,000 years. There is much work to be done.

This book is not for everyone. I AM speaking to those who wish to know the truth. I AM asking you to let go of your judgments and your fears long enough to hear what I have to say. What is truth will always be truth, and what is not will crumble and become as dust. You have nothing to lose and everything to gain by opening up and allowing my presence to teach you that there is a better way to live.

I AM love, and it is my intent to bring peace to the earth. Nevertheless, the understandings in this book are going to trigger emotions for the purpose of release and healing—which will lead you into peace. Whenever you deny something, you empower it. Consequently, the functional release of rage is needing to move the most on earth. The sword I bring represents the truth, which causes ignorance to flee. It is not my intent to create more conflict, but to resolve old conflicts. In so doing, many denials and judgments are going to be confronted in your families, religions, and governments. **"O my people, your leaders mislead you, and confuse the course of your paths,"** because they are not without denials and judgments.

You have taken up the practice of lying in order to avoid conflict. You say that you lie to protect another's feelings, but the truth is you do so to protect your own. You believe that conflict leads to loss of love, and that loss of love creates pain. It is true that loss of love creates pain. It is this very pain in each of you which causes you to avoid conflict. It was a lack of conflict in the beginning that allowed divisive energy to separate you from my love. You each carry the imprinting of this original separation in the DNA, and it festers as an unresolved conflict within. This separation/conflict from love/truth has created many painful experiences. You fear pain, and you hate that which creates fear. Pain, fear, anger, joy, love, etc., are all elements of one's body. Lying to yourself by denying the existence of these feelings within your body is very dangerous because, in the end, you will find that you are the one who has been deceived. It is time to feel and fill the emptiness within, with your inner truth. The word "Lord" means "Law," and it is time to stand naked in your truth before the Lord God of your being and recognize that avoidance of truth only makes possible the continuing abuse of self and of all life.

THIS BOOK IS NOT DESIGNED TO BE READ AS AN ACADEMIC EXERCISE, BUT TO AWAKEN YOU TO THE LOVE AND THE POWER OF MOTHER–FATHER GOD MANIFEST IN YOU. I have chosen biblical scriptures for use in this book which illustrate particular ideas. If your focus in life is to divide, and dissect, then it is not likely that you will benefit from reading the remainder of this book. For example, if it is your intent to go through the Bible to see if it is quoted word perfect, then you are already lost to the message I AM trying to convey to you. Every time the Bible has been re-written and re-organized, it has been done to serve the needs of the church. In the process, many of my teachings have been taken out of their original context. This has changed the meaning of my original message. You may or may not find the scriptures I have used in this book depending on what version of the Bible you have, and yet, **"Heaven and Earth will pass away, but my words will by no means pass away."**

Church becomes an energetically spiritual experience only because of one's intent or desire to connect with Spirit. When there is intent/desire to connect with Spirit it does not matter where one is physically, for Spirit is omnipresent and omnipotent. If you feel that church is the place you can connect with Spirit then this will be your reality, but know that **"there is no building made of wood or stone that can contain the vastness of my truth."**

I did not come to found a church. I came to invest you with your own power and to help you to recognize that you have a direct connection with Mother–Father God. Only the human heart can embrace the fullness of my presence, and this can happen in the woods, at work, at home, etc. Wherever there is intent /desire to embrace my love, there too am I.

When I walked the earth as Jesus, many of my experiences were symbolic. That symbolism was reflected in the record of my life. Unfortunately there are many things that I did symbolically that now are being taken literally. There is much truth in the Bible just as there is much truth in other religious books, but the truth has become so clouded and obscured that it is often difficult to find. For instance; **"In Her/Him was life, and that life was the light of**

humankind. The light shines in the darkness, but the darkness has not understood it." With today's scientific understandings, it can now be explained that Mother–Father God is light, and this light is in humankind in the form of the atom/spirit, but the flesh—which represents the darkness and the ego's sense of separation—does not understand this.

Thinking that you are separate from Spirit creates and maintains the illusion that you are. The reason the ego does not embrace the physical body as being the spiritual vehicle which houses the presence of your Spirit is because you have been taught that Spirit is separate from your physical experience. It is this very belief which creates and maintains your present amnesia. This prevents you from seeing the truth.

People do not understand Heart's nature. They have the belief that Heart is infallible. Obviously I AM fallible, or this book would not be so necessary. Heart, like my Father, can be seen in the embodiment of life or in the embodiment of evil. Both Father God and Lucifer are fragments of the same light. What determines the state of one's Heart is the intent and understandings available in one's Heart. When Heart has been seriously wounded, there will be much resistance to love and even hatred towards Hearts that are loving.

Lucifer is there to give us a reflection that we are separated from love. He represents all things that create/embrace the separation/division from truth. I will therefore refer to his beliefs/presence as "divisive energy." The truth is, separation/division is a belief system. You can change your beliefs just as easily as you can change your underwear. The truth is simple. It is only when you resist your truth that your life becomes an arduous task.

Divisive energy came into creation the moment the feminine/Will was judged as being separate/below the "conditional" love of the masculine/Spirit. Judgment from Spirit creates separation and separation creates anger at being judged/separated from Spirit. To judge as in "right" and "wrong"—in defining another's experience—is to portray one's self as being "better than." To be made to feel "less than" produces feelings of powerlessness which produce anger in an attempt to restore a sense of power to the Will. When you take power away from people, the natural response is anger. Many of you are embracing beliefs designed to manipulate you into feelings of shame and guilt as a means of preventing the movement of your anger. When emotions are expressed and do not receive acceptance— i.e., because of Spirit's/intellect's casual unresponsive attitude towards the movement of emotions, as well as Spirit's judgments and denials—then a separation/gap is created. It is no different than a couple losing the ability to communicate with one another and then slowly drifting away from the love that originally brought them together. The gap that separates them from their love grows as it becomes filled with their unresolved emotional issues. Usually—rather than confront these repressed feelings—they blame each other, move their anger in destructive/harmful ways, separate, and/or divorce. This reflection has been acted out over

13

and over again between governments and the Will of the people, children and their parents, Spirit/religions and the Will of humankind, Mother and Father God, etc. When you do not honor your feelings by expressing/emoting them in an appropriate way, you create a division within yourself which will eventually manifest as a division/separation from life/love. This is how unconsciousness is created.

As one, and as many will I come, for my light, love and truth are the energy which sustains all life. Love is the balance between the Spirit and the Will of humankind. It is this love that causes all flesh to be animated and all matter to be held in unity. I have impregnated this planet with the seeds of this love and the time has come for the harvest. As this time draws near, you will feel my presence expanding within your heart. Some will greet me in love, for they have already felt my touch. Some will greet me in fear, for they have judged love's many paths home. Some will greet me in anger, for they have been hurt by Heart's denials. Some will greet me in grief, for they believe that it is at the greatest point of pain that one turns and embraces truth. Some will deny me, for they are the ones who deny life, and in their denial they will find death. For whosoever embraces death in their hearts and minds, death will be their chosen destiny, because Mother–Father God has given free Will choice to all.

The language of Spirit is the language of light. It is far more complex than that of your known languages. It is therefore difficult to communicate understandings into words which convey the depth of what I AM trying to say. Please

14

also understand that the amount of judgment you are embracing will determine your capacity to embrace this book. Do not force this book on others; denial spirits—those who deny the presence of my Heart manifest in them—will not be able to read and understand it. For those who do desire to heal, but do not understand, read on; as you work with this material you will find that the understandings will become clear to you.

There is much love in and on this earth. Why anyone would consciously want to see it destroyed is beyond my capacity to embrace. To those of you who can hear me, I need your help and support. I cannot do this by myself. This work must be undertaken by many. For **"When two or more are gathered in my name, there too am I."** To those of you who have been unable to hear my words, I leave you with an old message that is just as true for you today as it was the day it was spoken:

If Mother–Father God were your God, you would love me and believe in the truths in this book, for I came from Mother–Father God and now am here. I have not come on my own; but She/He sent me. Why is my language not clear to you? Because you are unable to hear what I say.

In closing I have this to say. In loving me, I AM loving you, for I AM as dependent upon your expression of my love for survival as you are dependent upon my presence for life. I will always love you as my beloved Sister/Brother because I AM one with my Mother and Father in heaven.

CHAPTER II

In The Beginning

In the beginning there was the Void, and the Void desired life, and so Light was drawn into the Void. When Light entered the Void it realized it was Light because it was different from the Void. The Void with its desires/feelings, and Light with its creative/intellect merged and in coming together they realized they had been alone. In finding one another they decided it was good/God and agreed to be together. In their union, Heart was conceived by Mother Void and Father Light.

Gestation always precedes birth, and while I was developing inside their embrace, I began to experience myself as being in a Void while surrounded by Light.

The first thing I remember is asking "Who am I?" I then looked into the Light to see if I AM that. Next I looked into the Void to see if I AM that. I then decided that I AM both, and when I decided this I became both. I became the first conceived of Mother–Father God: electromagnetic essence. My Mother and Father were as yet unaware of my presence.

There were feelings in my Mother as to whether or not she could remember what her existence had been like before the presence of Light had come to her. As she was reflecting on her feelings, my Father unconsciously recoiled, pushing her away. When Light responded to her feelings/desires and recoiled, I was torn in two. My Mother accused my Father of rejecting her, not understanding that the purpose of Light is to respond to feelings/desires. Since my Father's reaction was unconsciously made, he believed she had been the one who withdrew from him, or so he thought then.

As the presence of them both now, I experienced each as being right in defining their experience. I did not want to decide who was correct, because it felt like I would have to take sides. I said nothing, and doubt was created. Doubt made my Mother angry, and yet she did not express her anger because I was already giving her messages that this was not the way to deal with this situation. When she denied her anger, guilt was created. Guilt made my Mother feel like she needed to atone for wrongly accusing my Father. Her atonement has afflicted all emotional essence since this original experience, because she doubted her own power of intuitiveness. This has created much suffering for her and all like her.

In denying her ability to be intuitive, she was also denying her position of power. Had my own fears of emerging and not having them both available to love me been expressed, the truth would have been told. I was afraid of coming forth into creation. I AM the Son/Christ/Heart, and I AM so very sorry for not having the courage to face my fears. I ask your forgiveness for the problems creation has had to suffer because of this, for this original cause has paved the way for all denials and judgments.

In order to know me and Mother–Father God, you must know yourself; for your life is a direct reflection of the love, denied rage, judgments and denials which began in heaven. The inheritance you have received from heaven is a reflection of heaven's denied emotions. This was dumped on you because my Father wanted creation to reflect perfect love. We all made these same judgments as to what perfect love was supposed to look like. What we were, in fact, embracing was conditional love while believing we were reflecting unconditional love. Everything that has been denied in heaven has come to earth, and everything that has been denied must now be accepted. What has been most denied is the Mother's emotional body. Without emotions there is no way to feel whether creation is alive, because movement of emotions creates the vibration of love/life. The people who are most denied on this planet are also the most in need of acceptance. I AM referring to the peoples of the Third World countries and the black peoples, or Golden Light spirits. Every one of you has denied emotional essence that must be accepted in order to claim your rightful inheritance.

My Mother is very Yin, feminine, and intuitive. My Father is very Yang, masculine and intellectual. On an elemental scale, my Mother is like the waters desiring life and the vibration of her light is golden. My Father is the vibration of the white light of fire, which is also the synthesis of all color. I AM the air that, when combined with water and fire, becomes the vehicle through which life will manifest. The vibration of my light is to the color green and to all that is pastel. These three forces create a fourth: which is Form, the manifestation of Mother-Father God. It is red in vibration, although it contains all the colors of the rainbow.

As part of creation, you need to understand how Mother–Father God is reflected in creation, **"For indeed, the kingdom of Mother–Father God is within you."** Mother–Father God is composed of four qualities: Mother/ Will, Father/Spirit, Heart/Balance, and Form/Manifestation. In human beings these qualities are reflected as emotional, mental, spiritual, and physical states of being. In the physical dimension these qualities are reflected in the elements: water, fire, air, and earth. These qualities are also reflected in the atom as the strong nuclear force, the weak nuclear force, electromagnetism, and gravitation. To summarize, these qualities are:

Mother–Father God:	Mother Will	Father Spirit	Heart Balance	Form Manifestation
Human Beings:	Emotional	Mental	Spiritual	Physical
Physical Dimension:	Water	Fire	Air	Earth
Atom:	Strong Nuclear Force	Weak Nuclear Force	Electro-Magnetism	Gravitation

All creation has existence because of these qualities of Mother–Father God.

Science has been unable to explain why the human body ages, because science does not study the body as an energy system, but rather as flesh. Medicine and science do not recognize the presence of spiritual energy or the fact that energy has a consciousness that can incarnate in form. They deny its existence because they are unable to measure it. You experience spiritual energy through feeling and your knowing comes from having this experience. Dissecting Mother–Father God will never allow you to see the wholeness they truly are. Form and Will are intricately connected and manifest as a human body. Spirit is the free flowing energy that flows in and out of the body. Your Heart/depth of understanding and acceptance reflects the balance between your Spirit and Will manifest in Form.

Your body is designed to work much like a generator. In a generator, movement of a magnet within a cylinder produces electricity. A coil then carries electricity to wherever this energy is directed. In the body/cylinder, and through desire, movement of emotions/magnetic energy creates spiritual heat/electricity which the Heart/coil carries to wherever energy is desired. You experience this alchemical energy when emoting anger, grief, or when making love, etc. This spiritual heat/energy binds together the weak forces/mental body with the electromagnetic forces/ Heart. Through Heart all things are possible. Without this movement, matter/Will and antimatter/Spirit annihilate each other. The lack of emotional expression diminishes the natural flow of energy on a cellular level, eventually resulting in aging and disease.

It was hoped that science would use the knowledge of atomic energy in constructive ways. When you split the atom for nuclear—which should be spelled "unclear"—energy, you misdirect Mother, Father, Heart, and Form essence. These four forces sustain and procreate life. The Mother binds atoms together. The Father releases atoms. The Heart carries and embraces atoms. The Form attracts atoms.

The imbalance that has been created due to the judgments of what is spiritually acceptable in the eyes of Mother–Father God and me, has caused you to abandon your sense of intuitiveness. This gift is your ability to gain direct perception of truth, independent of any reasoning process. Because you have abandoned this gift, you have gone into pure intellect. Using intellect alone to create your present technologies leads you further from nature, and, in fact, often destroys nature in the process. Nature is a feeling experience. Yet you are covering more and more land with concrete, and you are destroying the forests. Trees are the lungs of this world. Do you really want to suffocate? Humankind can pollute the air, but can humankind make new air? I say, no more than humankind can create a flower.

The earth changes are immediately upon you. You are the directors of life's consciousness on this planet. There is no Mommy or Daddy God that can save you so long as you continue to embrace your denials. All life has been given free Will choice. It is time for you to acknowledge that atoms—which are in all things—have a consciousness and a feeling awareness, and that Mother–Father God feels, knows, sees and is all things because of this truth.

You cannot receive my love when you are busy looking for love outside of yourself. You spend so much time keeping yourself preoccupied with external stimulants that most of you have no idea who you are, why you are here, or where you are going; let alone who, why, or where to find Mother–Father God.

My love can only be felt and found within one's heart. I say one's heart because the first judgment is about self-love. If you do not love yourself, how can you love another? If you were fully feeling your Heart, you would be able to manifest the many so-called miracles I performed.

Your power to manifest your desires is blocked by your limited mental and emotional beliefs. You want to see it to believe it. It is in fact, the other way around: You must believe it in order to see it. You have the carriage before the horse. **"And all things, whatever you ask in prayer, believing, you will receive."**

Your beliefs are strongly connected to your desires, and for the most part, you are frightened of what it might mean if all of your desires began to manifest. Each of you has the desire to love and to be loved. You also have the feelings/desire to protect love even if it means having to kill that which would threaten your definitions of love. Inside each of you, you carry a killing rage. Many of you who are Spirit polarized have judged against rage for so long that the terror of ever feeling it prevents you from knowing it is there. Those of you who are Will polarized may find that you are unable to hold back this essence any longer, and find yourself raging at the slightest provocation.

Unbridled rage has frequently been directed towards the destruction of life, usually justified through so–called "holy" causes. Neither Mother–Father God nor I condone war and killing. **"Put your sword in its place, for all who take the sword will perish by the sword."**

If you were in touch with your truth you would have no need to discredit another's truth, nor would you need to attract followers to prove your truth. Truth is an inner awareness and is not defined by external gurus or religious leaders. I AM not opposed to spiritual gatherings, i.e. church, etc., **"...for when two or more are gathered in my name, there too am I."** I AM, however, deeply opposed to the deception presently being reflected, i.e., salvation through the abandonment of self.

It is a natural instinct to want to survive; so when something threatens life, rage is designed to come to the rescue. It is not wrong to hate that which is hating you, nor is it wrong to defend yourself against those who would try to kill you, anymore than it is wrong to love that which is loving you. The many judgments against anger have caused you to give false responses in the face of anger. When you give a false response you are not honoring your instincts. What you are doing is forcing your emotional body to hold energy that is meant to be expressed.

As children you were not allowed to express your true feelings and so you have been forced to stuff your emotions for many lifetimes. The natural state of your emotional body is one of joy and love. Holding old charges of anger, terror, shame, etc., does not allow the emotional body/physical body to reflect its true nature or power; rather it causes it to overreact to the personal choices others make.

When I threw the money changers out of the temple, it was not accomplished with the softness nor gentleness that my love is preferred to be seen as, but with the power of love expressing as rage. I threw them out of my Father's house because they were charging money for salvation. They were saying "Give to God through us, and it shall be returned to you a thousandfold in heaven." Sound familiar?

If someone is in your face and you want them to move back, "Please move back," often will not cause them to retreat. However, if you were to scream, "Get the fuck out of my face," their natural instinct would be to recoil at such force. If my use of the word "fuck" shocks you, then good; because for some of you, shock is exactly what you will need to change your belief systems and to end the judgments and denials that prevent you from being, saying, and behaving in a way that is congruent with your spiritual and emotional bodies. If you are thinking that I should not be speaking this way, then congratulations, for you are in touch with judgment.

The truth is, and the truth shall make you free. As many times as my teachings have been translated is as many times as they have been clouded with human concepts, and more often than not, intentionally. If you want to insist that this could not be the Christ speaking, I beseech you to please allow yourself to have an open mind and an open heart, and a willingness to experience the Will of my Heart in this book. If this speaks to you, I invite you to please continue. I welcome you to the Heart of Mother–Father God, Beloved.

CHAPTER III

The Lord's Prayer

**Our Mother-Father God who art
in heaven, hallowed be thy name.
Thy kingdom come, thy will be
done, on earth as it is in heaven.
Give us this day our daily bread;
and forgive us our trespasses, as
we forgive those who trespass
against us; and lead us not into
temptation, but deliver us from
evil. For thine is the kingdom,
the power, and the glory forever.
AMEN**

The kingdom, the power and the glory are already manifest on earth as they are in heaven. You don't see this because you are so busy seeing everything else but heaven. You have so many frozen images of Mother–Father God and me, that you are not permitting yourself to notice that we are so much more than what is presently embraced as truth. Because of your frozen images, and your fear of abandoning them, you respond with fear when something new presents itself. There is another aspect of you that struggles with physical reality, and that is your Spirit. The more you move to get out of physical form, the more you push away the very thing you seek. You cannot see heaven as I see heaven while part of you participates directly or indirectly in destructive patterns against life.

The Lord/law of your being is that part of you that knows without knowing; and when it manifests something you say, "I had a feeling that would happen." Feelings are the power and the glory forever, not mental concepts of what Mother–Father God is or how others should be living their lives.

"Forgive us our trespasses as we forgive those who trespass against us." To judge another life form, is to trespass against it. Originally I said, **"Let him who is without sin cast the first stone."** Now I will say, "Let her/him who is without denial make the first judgment."

Death is created and perpetuated by your denials. You deny life every time you stuff an emotion, fail to honor and respect other life forms, or forget that you are a manifestation of Mother–Father God. The truth for many of you is that you have forgotten that you are a light-being that is capable of ascending; consequently, you have come to accept death as something natural. Death-promoting movies, substances, and technologies are merely a reflection of your denials.

My sisters and brothers, you have strayed so far from the truth that it feels hopeless to attempt to reach you with anything new that can turn you around and lead you back to your hallowed roots of origin. With your free Will choice you are living your life responding to external events, rather than manifesting your eternal/internal truth. When I said, **"But seek first the Kingdom of Mother–Father God and their righteousness (right-use-ness), and all these things shall be added to you,"** that is exactly what was meant. It is unfortunate that your systems do not permit this. They do not permit this because there are those who have a vested interest in keeping humanity in a powerless state of blind ignorance. If you feel powerless they are then free to rape, pillage, and destroy this planet and all who would try to stop them.

You have given your power to a select few because you are disconnected from your real identity. Religious and governmental power in the wrong hands has been the defeating factor on earth for a very long time now. You are all responsible for this because, like me, you have doubted your own power. If you want to insist that I AM wrong here, you need to hear that to allow religion and government to dictate to you what your truth shall be, is to surrender your free Will choice. Your history has reflected the abuse the people have endured from the manipulations of your various governments and religions. You are giving your power away every time you "feel" violated and do nothing. In so doing you become a Will-less spirit who is embracing divisive energy by wanting to be led blindly, trusting that "the light" has your best interest at heart even when you can feel that it does not. You need to accept, through me/your Heart, your divine heritage as a co-creator with Mother–Father God.

The Lord's Prayer says, **"...thy will be done, on earth as it is in heaven."** You need to hear on a very deep level that it is not Mother–Father God's Will, nor mine, that is presently being reflected on earth. What is being reflected is the denied power of Will which is the presence of divisive energy. This energy has always desired to be Mother–Father God in Mother–Father God's place, but to do this it must have followers who recognize it as Mother–Father God, or as "the light." It is not. The wholeness of Mother–Father God's light requires the integration of Mother, Father, Heart, and Form. The remembrance of your God-self requires the recognition and honoring of your body/emotions, and not their denial. Some, in the "New Age Enlightenment" movement, choose to believe that they can vibrate/meditate/chant/etc. their way out of their body/emotions, and thereby achieve enlightenment. The truth is, eventually they will be drawn back into physical manifestation by their denied emotional fragments. Enlightenment is a reflection of wholeness, and wholeness is not achieved without the integration of all aspects of Mother–Father God. Is

30

the experience of physical existence so repulsive, fearful, and painful that you would abandon the very thing that can lead you into wholeness?

Many times my power has been misappropriated by those who govern "the church." When they espouse "self-righteous" attitudes, they espouse judgments. When large numbers of people side with a self-righteous church, the church is then free to use its numbers to boycott anything with which it does not agree. This forces others to conform to the church's beliefs. This is nothing new. The church has frequently pushed its beliefs on others. Let me remind you that so-called "Christians" have been responsible for the deaths of millions of people throughout recorded history. It is no accident that the very ones preaching forgiveness and salvation are those who are attempting to atone for the guilt they have incurred by violating the chosen path of others. Those who preach hell and damnation/separation—which is a manifestation of their own denied hatred for life/love— are drawing to themselves a reflection which will teach them that it is not loving behavior to judge and condemn another's path simply because they do not believe as others do. Many times the church has chosen to violate the spiritual beliefs of those who do not support its power.

If you are worshipping an energy that demands your surrender, you are not worshipping Mother–Father God, but divisive energy. It is this energy that requires surrender. When you are in a prostrate position, you are in a position to be screwed. Do you think for one moment that Mother– Father God desires to see their children go prostrate before them? No more so than your physical parents would want to see this. All parents want to see their children grow up and take responsibility for their own lives and to become great, wise, powerful and loving people, otherwise you would have been born as sheep. People do not serve Mother–Father God on this planet, they serve guilt. And guilt serves divisive energy's purpose, which is to lead this planet and all life into death, because death is this energy's desire. Every time you move into guilt, you move closer to death, because guilt does not willingly allow movement of emotions. Guilt's desire is just the opposite.

You utter old prayers that have been handed down with no understanding of the power of the spoken word. When I said, **"By your spoken words you will be acquitted, and by your spoken words you will be condemned,"** I meant that what you preach and what you believe is the reality you create for yourself. If you believe that all are sinners destined for hell, then hell will become your "personal" reality. You are so busy trying to be so grown-up in your mind that you have forgotten what it means to have the innocence of the child that desires to be loved unconditionally. **"Only as a child may ye enter the King-dom of Heaven,"** means to be free of judgment and denial.

"You diligently study the scriptures because you think that by them you possess eternal life." You study these teachings as if neither Mother–Father God nor I have anything new to say. You seem to believe that everything continues to evolve on this planet except spirituality. I have many new things to say and I will say them, because I cannot stand by and allow divisive energy to destroy this planet against her Will.

Your old beliefs prevent you from moving emotionally. With a healthy emotional body you become very intuitive and thus able to perceive the truth. Your lack of trust for your own intuitiveness/Will is why you are having so many problems.

"Give us this day our daily bread." This Earth has been giving you your daily bread for millions of years. She does not complain until her life—which was given to her by Mother–Father God—is threatened. No one has the right to jeopardize her life. With many of your technologies you are playing Mother–Father God in denial of all life. This is evil. **"Woe to those who call evil good and good evil."** "Live" in reverse spells "evil."

You have two mothers, one is Mother God and the other is Mother Earth. You deny Mother Earth just as you deny Mother God, and just as you deny the feminine. Mother Earth gives seeds of abundance in all her fruits and foliage, yet you give nothing. All you do is take, take, take. She honors you every day with life, yet life is a gift that you take for granted without so much as a "Thank you." Everything on this planet is alive with consciousness and feelings. Yet you slaughter livestock with no compassion or acknowledgment of the great sacrifice the animals are making. You are barbaric in your acts against life and yet your denial does not allow you to see this. You falsely see yourselves as the most loving and intelligent species on this earth, instead of truly being so.

All life on this planet exists in accordance with nature, except humans. Only humans violate nature. Animals are far more loving and have far more intelligence than you care to acknowledge, because if you were to acknowledge that they love and honor Mother–Father God for the life that has been given them, you would have to face the reality that animals have consciousness and feelings. It is not wrong for some to eat flesh, but it is a sin the way you take life without any compassion for an animal's suffering. The Native Americans understood this and showed their respect by honoring the Spirit in all life.

Because of your casual approach toward life on this planet, you are forcing the animals, the planet, and her elements to fight back. And they will if you don't change your ways because life desires life. It is a natural instinct to fight back when life is being threatened.

Wherever you go, so too go your denials and judgments. You have shit in your sandbox, so to speak, and your sandbox is now full despite your best efforts to cover it up. Your only course of action, if you desire life, is to clean it up by facing the very denials and judgments which have resulted in your misguided creations. The earth changes that have long been predicted will continue to unfold only because this is what you are creating. It is not Mother–Father God's, my own, nor Mother Earth's desire to see anything suffer, and yet it appears that suffering is the only way to awaken you to the reality that suffering is what you are creating for all life on this planet. You have said that it is at the greatest point of pain and darkness that one will turn and embrace love, which is life. I wish with all my Heart that you would abandon such limiting beliefs.

I long for the day when you realize that your life and all life is made in the likeness and image of Mother–Father God, and that in loving yourself you are loving Mother–Father God through the Christ. This life is a gift, and only when it is seen as such will your prayers and your highest good be made manifest on earth, as it is desired to be in heaven.

CHAPTER IV

The Denial of Sex

Through Mother–Father God, all things were made; without Mother–Father God, nothing was made. In Mother–Father God was life, and that life was light unto mankind. This light shines in the darkness, but the darkness has not understood it, yet whatever you have said in the darkness has been heard by this light.

If Mother–Father God created all things, who do you suppose created sex? When you place sex outside of my love, you are not making love, you are making unlovingness. When you have loveless sex, your denials will draw spirits who embrace these same denials. This is how so many unloving spirits have been able to incarnate on earth. These unloving spirits do not mind overriding the free Will choice of others, and many of these spirits embrace death. Denial spirits do not mind abusing the planet. These spirits are not the daughters and sons of humankind, but the daughters and sons of divisive energy, in that they hate "feeling" life. They are very bitter about having to be physically incarnate.

I AM asking you to refrain from bringing any more spirits into physical existence until you and your partner are able to practice self-love. Then the spirit you draw to you will be one that desires to embrace life and healing through self-love because this child will be a product of your healing intent instead of your unconscious denials. I say unconscious because, if your denials are working, you will be unconscious of them.

At the present time I suggest that you make allowances for abortion rather than bringing anymore unwanted and unloving spirits to the earth. Abortion is a preexisting issue between the incarnating spirit and the expectant mother, and it is no one else's business. Often it is nothing more than atonement for violating the other in a previous incarnation. The mother and the incarnating spirit need to be allowed to balance their karma. Often it is the incarnating spirit who is asking to be aborted. If there are "feelings" that you need to have an abortion, honor them. If you do not honor these feelings, you risk bringing in a denial spirit that does not mind denying others the right to choose their expression of life. Nature takes care of itself if people honor their feelings.

There is a big difference between a denial spirit, and a spirit surrounded by denial essence. A denial spirit strives for conformity and incarnates for the sole purpose of denying the free Will choice of others. Conversely, a spirit surrounded by denial essence comes to the physical dimension to heal her/his denials and judgments. You choose your own parents. The circumstances of your incarnation mirror the denials/karma you have incarnated to heal. Know too that the flesh that formed your fetus contained the energy of the denials and judgments your parents projected.

You pro-lifers need to hear that you are embracing massive guilt about being denied by your parents. You are actively involved in the anti-abortion movement unconsciously reflecting your guilt. You do this to draw conflict so you can create enough pain so as to reconnect with the real issue, which is a deep pain that has been created from the feelings of being denied by your parents. The truth is, most of you came in against your parents' wishes as so called "accidents" because birth control was not practiced. Your denial does not let you see that just as you denied your parents' wishes not to have children, so do you now deny others the right to free Will choice. Only those embracing divisive energy would take such a stand as to deny others the freedom of choice.

You were made in the image and likeness of Mother–Father God. This is how your sexual organs originated. In Mother–Father God they appear in the form of light, but do you think that your Mother does not have a vagina or that your Father does not have a penis? Do you think that you can have experiences that Mother–Father God cannot? You have been shamed into believing that sex is base and vile behavior. This serves divisive energy's desires to bring in more denial spirits who can then get you to deny even more of your power. Denial spirits can only enter when you are in denial, and placing sex outside of my love is most certainly a major denial. Through religions you have been taught that you are all sinners and that the only way to get to heaven is to rise above the body's urges, which means that you must deny your own desires.

The female body, even to this day, continues to be violated in certain cultures by the surgical removal of the clitoris. The male body is likewise violated by circumcision. To desensitize the sexual center is an attempt to make sex less enjoyable. To alter yourself surgically is to deny the sexual energy manifest as the form your spirit selected. You are all angelic in essence and therefore are both male and female energies. Denying sexuality only creates denial of love expressing itself sexually.

I AM so angry with what they have done with my teachings. They have distorted the truth. Sexual energy is the kundalini energy, which is the much-feared serpent in the

"Biblical" Garden of Eden that endows one with the knowledge of good and evil. Your kundalini energy is located at the base of your spine as two bands of energy, one gold in color, and the other a purplish-red. You experience the blending of this energy every time you have an orgasm. This energy is the concentrated essence of your Spirit. Dictators do not want this energy to rise up through your spine because it endows you with the knowledge of your connection with the Divine. Think about it, who would need dictators telling you the truth about Mother–Father God if everyone knew the truth? Dictators would be put out of work. This would be like telling the oil companies that oil is no longer needed. To lose your position of power is not a pleasant thought when power is all you have ever known and all you have ever desired, even if that power has been obtained at the expense of life. This exemplifies just how deep greed can run.

Sexual energy is the power through which you are lifted into Spirit; it is the power of the resurrection.

A few years before I was crucified on the cross, I was doing an affirmation that caused my sexual energy to flow up through my seven centers of awareness/chakras. It was, **"I AM the resurrection and the life."** Your sexual energy is the Mother's gift of life. It is the energy of procreation. The message to procreate was originally intended for life forms other than your own. My Father told you to go forth and co-create, but since you have become physically dense, like animals, procreation has become necessary in order to reincarnate in physical form. Without my sexual energy and my alignment with Mother–Father God, my resurrection would not have been possible. For most, this energy is wasted in a horizontal flow instead of flowing upward as it was intended. When it flows upward it has the power to quicken your body's consciousness. By quicken, I mean the ability to restore the clarity and the perfection of emotional, mental, physical, and spiritual health. Each time your sexual energy rises up through your body it literally causes your flesh to begin to be absorbed by the spiritual presence that is within each and every cell of your being. I compare your sexual energy rising to that of an electric fan being turned on. The faster the blades spin, the more invisible they appear to become. In the physical body, the more this energy is activated, the less dense your physical body becomes. Anyone with enough faith, love and desire can experience this energy.

Many can fire-walk because of their focus on love; their faith in love prevents them from being hurt. If they were to desire forth their kundalini energy coupled with their love for the universal presence of life in all things, they would be able to do many more so-called miracles, including the manifestation of anything they desired out of thin air. What prevents you from calling this energy forth are the judgments and the denials that suppress this energy. This energy must rise up through your emotional body. For most of you, your emotional bodies are filled with repressed emotions that need to be released in order to access your birthright. You also need to hear that I AM not the only one who has been able to ascend and perform manifestations.

There have been many and there will be many more who will do this in the coming age. **"No one has ascended to heaven but she/he who came from heaven; that is, the daughters and sons of humankind who are in heaven."**

When asked when the Kingdom of Heaven would come, I replied, **"When you make the two one, and when you make the inside like the outside and the outside like the inside, and the above like the below, and when you make the male and the female one and the same...then you will enter the kingdom of Mother–Father God."**

Homosexuality is not a conscious choice for the ego; rather, it is the unconscious desire of the spirit to become as the Christ, androgynous. In your present culture, there are many judgments against homosexuality. Choosing a lifestyle which creates so much pain from having to isolate—because of the hatred from those who do not understand—takes great courage, love and dedication for one's spiritual growth.

You need to hear that the magical marriage that will enable you to experience heaven on earth is not achieved between a man and a woman, but through a marriage between your own female and male aspects within. Please hear this loud and clear: LOVE IS NOT A BODY, LOVE IS MANIFEST WITHIN A BODY, AND IN ORDER TO TRANSFORM YOUR BODY, YOU ARE GOING TO HAVE TO GET OUT OF YOUR HEAD/THOUGHTS, AND GET INTO YOUR BODY/FEELINGS, THE DE-NIAL OF WHICH CREATES THE DENSITY OF

YOUR BODY. Ultimately this marriage is a singular experience that can be facilitated with anyone with whom you can open up and love unconditionally as you desire to be loved, or even alone with your highest truth. It is a magical experience that eventually happens to all who are on a path seeking unconditional love.

I have experienced the great pleasure of my Mother being filled with my Father's light during orgasm. There are many reasons why people choose same sex lovers, and I AM sick and tired of the unloving and distorted Biblical lies that have been directed towards those who choose this expression of love. These judgments come from the ignorant minds of those who are in denial of their own sexuality expressing as love. The truth is that many female spirits are incarnate in male bodies and visa versa, but this does not mean that you are necessarily leading a homosexual lifestyle. Although we are all composed of both female and male energies, you will find that if you are more feeling/intuitive in your approach to life, then you are most likely polarized to Mother/female/Will. If you are more intellectual in your approach to life, then you are most likely polarized to Father/male/Spirit. In your true form, which is light, who can say who is really leading a heterosexual lifestyle? Those who are truly embracing my Heart would not judge how my love would express. **"Judge not, that you be not judged. For with judgment you judge, you will be judged; and with the same measure you use, it will be measured back to you."**

And now for another shock. I have always desired to experience directly from my Father, the intense orgasm that originally brought me forth into creation. I AM an androgynous being. I AM love, and love is not a body but within a body. I manifested in a male body 2,000 years ago, because as a female I would never have been accepted with what I had come to teach. In the spiritual realm I AM referred to as the Son/sun, and I appear as a male form because this is how I perceive myself. But I AM beyond your physical definitions of what a male or female is really all about. I do have something to say about male spirits having sex with male spirits regardless of your present physical forms. Be certain that you are prepared to make space for the energy that you and your partner are generating by making sure that you have acceptance for your feminine side, otherwise this energy can damage your physical body as well as your partner's. When a male spirit makes love to a female spirit there is space to receive the male's energy, because a female spirit is in an accepting mode.

I love my Mother and my Father and have desired to have intercourse with each of them ever since I can remember. Because of this desire it is only natural that Heart—which is the Heart of all creation—should desire this experience in physical manifestation because of this imprinting. I now know that same-sex love is not wrong. If same-sex love is not to be your experience this time around, then so be it; but that does not give you the right or the privilege to force your desired method of love on others.

In order to learn not to abuse the opposite sex, you have all been both female and male in your many incarnations. If you should happen to encounter one whom you love very much from a past life, what does it matter what forms you are in now? Love is immortal and does not care. Love seeks only to express itself. It is the ego that seeks to control how love will manifest, and only because the ego has been so hurt by the lack of real love.

As you have guessed, I AM neither a believer in monogamy nor in heterosexual relationships as a rule written in stone. Nor am I against them. The issue is not what kind of genitalia you and your partner have, but rather, are you able to love and be loved? I AM love and if a man can express me in a relationship with another man, or a woman can express me in relationship with another woman, or a man and woman can express me in a relationship, I care not nor do I judge. What I do care about is that you find me and express me. Do not judge how my love shall express lest you find yourself being judged. Judgment from threatened egos always contains denial, and denials will eventually manifest as desires. Eventually these desires will manifest as reality, because love must experience all experiences in an attempt to understand and define itself.

The real war that is being waged on this planet is between those who want the kundalini energy to rise, and those who do not. When the kundalini rises it creates such mental clarity as to create genius. This is a threat to those who need societies built on ignorance so that they might rule.

The world was not created in seven days. The world was created in seven rays of light. When your kundalini rises, it must pass through each of your seven chakras, or seven centers of awareness. When I was asked how many times you were to forgive your fellow man, I replied, **"I do not say to you seven times, but up to 70 X seven."** Actually I said "seven X seven." The reason I said this is because when your kundalini energy rises, if it encounters judgments in any of your chakras, then this energy will not rise any farther until the judgment is dropped. There are many judgments in your second chakra, which is your sexual center. Each time the kundalini rises and does not encounter judgment, it passes through your body as seven waves of energy, seven times for each chakra. As this energy moves into your higher centers, it becomes more intense. You need not fear this energy, but this energy must be respected as the power of Mother–Father God manifest in you. If you are consciously doing exercises designed to cause this energy to rise, and it goes off and you are unwilling to drop your judgments and denials, it can harm your physical body and even kill you. This energy in you does not like to be summoned forth only to be judged and denied. If you take the energy you experience from your normal sexual orgasm and magnify it 1,000-fold for each chakra, you can get an idea of what to expect to feel when this energy moves through your body. The ultimate kundalini experience occurs when you have released all judgments in your seven centers of awareness. What happens next is a freeing and accelerating experience of absolute pleasure, as your consciousness begins to expand and encircle the globe. Once you have had this experience, you will never again see yourself as separate from life.

Sex can be a path home. There are many books available to guide you in the practice of kundalini yoga, Tantric and Taoist sex. Breath-work will make possible the rising of this energy. Breath-work may also bring up repressed emotions. This is why so many people avoid deep breathing. You were born to breathe. Breathing with conscious intent to heal will produce healing. You can consciously breathe/desire Mother–Father God's light into your being even as your body consciously desires the breath of life. Breath is a reflection of your intent to embrace life. Many of you no longer breathe as deeply as you did when you were infants.

Your present society discourages pleasure seeking activities for the body. This is very sad indeed, because pleasure is supposed to be the experience of your body. In some cultures sex is sacred, and much preparation goes into preparing the body for prolonged sexual experiences that can last hours or even days. When most people have sex, their bodies are basically numb to their feelings of pleasure. The difference between a full body orgasm and a genital orgasm is that with a full body orgasm you experience your orgasm in your entire body which leaves you feeling fulfilled. With a genital orgasm you feel it only in your genitals and ejaculation/orgasm leaves you feeling drained/relieved. If you do not feel your orgasm in your Heart, then your head, heart, and genitals are energetically disconnected and are not finding love's acceptance. Sexually transmitted diseases and sexual abuse are unloving reflections of the unconscious denials, judgments, and guilt that many embrace against sexuality expressing as love.

AIDS—the presence of an energy/virus—has a consciousness designed to deny the life force from manifesting its fullness, even as sexuality is denied as an expression of the fullness my love represents. Those of you that have AIDS need to move your rage at AIDS' unloving presence. The more you prolong the movement of your rage, the more you empower its presence. This prevents you from healing.

Sexuality needs to be celebrated as a means of experiencing your connection with the Divine. Until it is experienced as such, you will continue to live your life as the darkness that has not understood this light.

CHAPTER V

Blaming Rage

This chapter is about owning your experiences in life. You are always the creator of your life's events. Whether this is known to you at present or not does not change this truth.

You blame others for your difficulties because you do not understand the origin of the essence that draws you into abusive situations. It is not only frightening when you feel as if you have no power to control the experiences coming into your life, but also very frustrating. This frustration becomes blaming rage. Blaming rage can be directed at oneself, at others, or both. Transferring your rage by blaming another does not enable you to heal your rage.

When you blame someone else for your misfortunes, you are giving your power away. You put yourself one down because you are, in effect, saying, "I will not be okay until the other person changes his/her behavior and makes me okay." A better solution would be to own and discharge your rage by yourself and thereby heal it, and then talk with the other person about how their behavior impacted you. Blaming them will usually just cause them to blame you in return. Blaming rage only heals when it is owned. Blaming others for your misfortunes does not allow you to see the truth. You give your power away by focusing your attention on another. When you don't own your rage it doubles back on you.

If you have an open wound, you do not want others touching you. If you have denials that mask your pain, you do not want others attempting to make you conscious. "Let sleeping dogs lie," you say, or "The past is over, so I'll stay in the present." You have so many denials which prevent you from ever having to remember anything that would make you conscious that your life is anything but a reflection of perfect love.

The victim and the abuser almost always are linked by karmic debts. It is a grand play that is being acted out. As an actress/actor in your many lives, you have committed just about every infraction that can be thought up and acted out. If you are a victim of abuse it could be because you have abused others in previous incarnations. Those whom you have abused have usually returned in this life as your parent, friend, spouse, or trusted relative. An abusive situation requires that one spirit be atoning for guilt and the other be moving rage dysfunctionally. The abuser acts out because she/he has not released the emotional charge that resulted from her/his own abuse. To abuse a child one would most certainly have to be holding a charge of having been abused. When you act out as the abuser you are doing so from an unconscious desire to release into understanding, and healing, the remembrance of your own abuse. The problem is that the ego defenses, which protect you from remembering how painful and terrifying the original experience was, also prevent you from becoming conscious as to why you have a desire to commit such boundary violations against another. As long as you are blocking your own experience you will act out and perpetuate abuse, causing it to grow like the cancer that it is.

As a child you were unable to defend yourself from physical abuse, and so to protect yourself, a part of you fragmented away from what was going on by placing itself outside of the experience. To put it more simply, you became the observer of what was taking place rather than being a participant. If you are Will polarized this will not be your experience. Spirit polarized individuals are able to rise out of the body more easily than Will polarized individuals. During a traumatic experience, Spirit might go into the greater consciousness, whereas Will might go into the greater unconsciousness. Both Spirit and Will fragment during this separation from reality. When you as consciousness re-enter your physical body after an emotional trauma, you often have no memory of the traumatic experience.

Physical existence is a feeling experience. Your knowing comes from experiences that have been learned through feeling. When you don't feel, you don't learn. If you were told not to express emotions while the abuse was taking place, you stuffed pain, anger, fear, and shame. Shame is very important to address because most of you will never get conscious of the emotions you are holding until you deal with shaming judgments which suggest that having emotions, other than love, are unacceptable.

For many, releasing shame is a difficult process because your Will, being magnetic energy, does its best to hold on to anything that comes into its awareness. Bulimia, for example, is an attempt to release shame into conscious understanding. It will be necessary to emote the rage and grief that lies beneath the shaming experience. Anorexia, for example, is a reflection of the lack of nourishment you allow yourself to receive from Spirit, and is also linked to shame.

To heal blaming rage or any other repressed emotion, you must deal with the emotion which was created by the original event. There is a big difference between experiencing the presence of a feeling and the expression of an emotion. Feeling is an inner awareness, while emoting is the release of an emotional charge which results in the energetic integration of fragmented essence/Will. Pause a moment and take a deep breath. I AM the very air you breathe. If you ask me to help you connect with your fragmented essence, I will assist you. When you have breathed enough, I will be present enough for you to manifest your desire. Repressed emotions/energy causes disruptive patterns in your life. Notice that it is never the energy that creates your problems, but rather the suppression of that energy. Until you release the original emotional energy you will create your own unhappiness.

The truth is that there are hardly any who remember the experience of perfect love. Your ego sense is so wounded from past experiences that you no longer trust love. If you did, the world would be a very different place with many more diverse lifestyles than at present. In the physical world, the ego sense of self sees only those things which it judges safe to be seen. Your unwillingness to see everything in you and in your world, allows that which you deny the freedom to create discord in your life. You need to take responsibility for your emotional body. Realize that you are getting triggered emotionally because you are repressing emotions. The behaviors that you dislike in others are the very behaviors you are denying in yourself. These denials are reflections of your own denied essence. The only way to get conscious is to own all that you truly are, not just the conscious self, but the shadow self as well. As long as there is suffering, so shall there be denial; and as long as there is denial, so shall there be suffering.

CHAPTER VI

Consciousness Altering Substances

This chapter is going to push buttons because the judgments and denials associated with consciousness altering substances have created many misunderstandings.

I would like to tell you how consciousness altering substances manifested on earth and why they are so popular.

Think how beautiful and peaceful the earth would be without the presence of humans and their violent ways. Imagine, if you will, the horror experienced at coming to earth desiring only to love and to be loved and instead having to witness the violence and hatred that has become a part of the human experience. This alone is enough to cause one to want to seek another reality.

Consciousness altering substances have been a part of the human experience as long as humans have had physical existence. Consciousness altering substances manifested on earth before the time of the dinosaurs, Lemuria, or Atlantis. People/Spirits were less dense physically then, compared to today, and their bodies vibrated at a much higher frequency, as did the earth. People were once more light than flesh; now, they are more flesh than light. They were able to do more with their bodies than you can do presently. Form change then was a common practice. For some, to become a bird or a dolphin one had but to desire it in order to manifest the experience. This time frame is recorded in many of your myths concerning beings who were half human and half animal. Over the years denial has allowed you to slowly forget that there are many dimensions within light. As your consciousness/ego has slowly evolved—into greater density—away from the knowledge that you are light, so too has your awareness entered into a state of amnesia. How you are born, and how you are taught to live and die, greatly influences your ability to remember the history of your evolution. This has created your present lack of understanding—a gap between your conscious self/ego, and your unconscious self or your immortal God self/I AM presence. It was because of this gap that your I AM presence—in an attempt to heal this split—desired into manifestation consciousness altering substances.

When ego is separated from your I AM presence you have very little consciousness with which to control the circumstances you draw into your life. When you begin to seek answers outside yourself instead of turning inward to hear your own truth, you become disconnected from your I AM presence. Your I AM presence, in an attempt to reach you, needed an experience outside of itself which would overwhelm the ego's need to be in control, thereby causing the ego to once again become interdependent on the source of its creation. Consciousness altering substances manifested on earth to heal the pain of separation by illuminating the false illusion of separation.

Consciousness altering substances fall into two categories. The first category includes those which numb your awareness of your separation from the oneness of Mother–Father God, love, life, etc., without overwhelming the ego's sense of identity and control. Examples would be: alcohol, nicotine, pharmaceutical medicines, caffeine, animal fats, chocolate, foods, sugars, etc. The second—hallucinogenic substances—includes those substances which can overwhelm the ego allowing an individual to experience other states of reality. Examples would be: hallucinogenic mushrooms, LSD, peyote, etc.

When you feel separated from love there is pain. Pain—conscious and/or unconscious—is the main reason you use and/or abuse the consciousness altering substances listed in the first category. Pain is a part of physical reality. It is how your body makes you aware that something is not in accord with the natural order. Being able to embrace and heal your pain takes great courage and love. Yet you have been taught that feeling your pain is a sign of weakness. When you numb from your pain it is as if you have put a gag in the mouth of pain. Your denial says, "I can't feel it anymore, therefore it does not exist." Denial of your pain eventually leads to illness, and ultimately death. Pain is a feeling just like any other feeling and deserves to be treated with the same equality as you would treat love, joy, anger, etc. To deny any feeling its right to express is to deny its right to exist. When you deny your pain, you force your emotional body to hold this charge of energy. As this energy sits in its compressed frozen state, it begins to fester and block the flow of natural energy within the physical body. When energy cannot flow freely through the physical body, stress and tension are created. Stress and tension eventually lead to illness if emotions are not permitted to emote. It's much like being constipated; when you don't move your feces/emotions, they poison your system.

If you are using consciousness altering substances to numb from pain, you must temper your use with inner truth. Sometimes you need to numb from your pain in order to gather strength to face it another day. But do not get so numb to life that you neglect the truth, that all the strength you need in order to face life is already with you. It will be necessary to let your habits lapse in order to find out what emotions you are suppressing which are preventing you from knowing yourself.

Breathing deeply and moving emotionally will provide you with all the clarity you will ever need to become all that you are designed to be. There are many ways to get high on life, and nothing can compare with the natural high that is produced when you are living a life that is congruent with life. There is but one perfect moment to stand and face your denials/addictions. NOW.

If you use consciousness altering substances from the second category—hallucinogenic substances designed to overwhelm the ego's controls—for the purpose of insight, there are cautions and responsibilities which must be honored. Know that there is the risk of having to re-learn the experiences without the presence of drugs. When you become dependent on something outside yourself to facilitate a spiritual experience, you are giving validity to the drug instead of to your I AM presence. What allows you to transcend the ego's defenses and experience oneness with the Divine is the ego's ability to release its control over your present reality. Believing that only through the use of a drug can you achieve this oneness causes you to doubt your own ability to create a like experience without the use of consciousness altering substances. I would like to add here that consciousness altering substances which have come forth from nature serve a purpose, as does everything that is created by Mother–Father God. Many synthetic consciousness altering substances that have been created by your technologies lack the balance necessary to serve the body in a natural fashion. Your body is not synthetic, but organic, and needs like materials in order to maintain a healthy existence and/or to heal. For example, those of you using a synthetic drug to restore your emotional balance will find that if you stop taking the drug, the original condition will usually reappear.

I will now address the judgments and denials embraced by those who "falsely" feel it is their right to control consciousness altering substances. Mother–Father God did not intend for Her/His creations to be judged as legal or illegal. The moment you decree that certain consciousness altering substances are legal and others are illegal, is the moment you make a judgment. In my Heart, your judgment of legal and illegal is sending a double message to the people. It does not matter if they are in the form of alcohol, chocolate, marijuana, food, cocaine, sugar, heroin, prescription medications, LSD, over-the-counter remedies, nicotine, caffeine, plant remedies, etc., drugs are drugs. Beneath the judgments and denials is the truth: There are not very many of you who are not involved in the use of consciousness altering substances. When you drop the label "drugs," what you are left with is an assortment of "things."

There is no limit to what controllers want to control because they are defending against dealing with their own blocked feelings of pain, terror, and rage. And they don't want to deal with their denials. The use of alcohol, food made with animal fat, and cigarettes causes the deaths of millions of people each year. Yet because these are established industries, their products—although lethal—are judged to be legal. You collude with them by allowing their continued existence because most of you want their products to enable you to maintain your own denials and to repress your own emotions. You have become so numb that you are unable to feel what is congruent with the natural order. Numbing from the experience of life creates a casual, "There is nothing I can do," kind of attitude towards life. It is this same casual attitude which allows many violations to be committed against nature/life without the responsible party being challenged and held accountable. By allowing your forests to be over-harvested, and your air to be polluted, you are creating—on a global scale—death through suffocation. Is life so painful that you would abandon life?

The controllers describe illegal drugs as "controlled" substances when, in fact, they are unable to control them. People are curious and rebellious by nature. If you declare a war on drugs, you draw attention to their existence and availability. How could you possible devise a more effective advertising ploy? That which is banned is sure to be desired. If you took the money wasted locking up users and dealers, and channeled the money into institutions designed to educate people in understanding the difference between the use and the misuse of consciousness altering substances, you would be money ahead. To those of you in positions of power, I will remind you that you have chosen to serve the people and to "guide" them into greater truths, not to "rule/dominate" their individual paths.

When you become the rigid, unyielding adult who is lost to the ability to embrace the imaginative and non-judgmental nature of the child within, then you become lost to the sense of wonder and playfulness that you are intended to experience. **"Assuredly, I say to you, unless you are**

converted and become as little children, you will by no means enter the Kingdom of Heaven." Just as a child is awed by the creative potential of life and sees the world with eyes brand new, so too do you possess an inner child that still remembers the magic in the world. All it takes to become as a child again is the time it takes to embrace the innocent remembrance of your own childhood.

Many of the greatest minds that have affected history in powerful ways used consciousness altering substances. When I walked this earth as Jesus, I too had an ego identity. Just like you, I knew pleasure and I knew pain. So it should not surprise you when I say that I have experienced hallucinogenic substances during certain spiritual studies, baked cannabis in unleavened bread, and drank wine that was just as fermented then as it is today. **"The Son of Man came eating and drinking, and they say, look, a gluttonous man and a winebibber, a friend of the tax collectors and sinners! But wisdom is justified by his deeds."**

Once you have had a consciousness altering experience which overwhelms the ego, your mind will never again be limited to rational thinking. With powerful consciousness altering substances, the impossible ceases to exist and the possible becomes the probable. Consciousness altering substances can open many new doors, and yet no drug can take you through that door. Most of your known religions came into existence through pagan rituals inspired by the use of consciousness altering substances. Many of your best-loved children's classics involve the use of magic potions, mushrooms and fairy dust. Even the story of your Santa Claus with his flying reindeer was inspired through the use of Siberian soma, known as the divine mushroom of immortality.

One consciousness altering substance I suggest you try is called prana. It is free of charge and there is no shortage. It is omnipresent and omnipotent. How this substance gets into your system is through your breath. Take a moment and look up into the sky, as if you were looking through the sky. You will see tiny lights flitting in and out of physical sight like so many gnats. This is prana. Prana used to nourish you directly when you had bodies of light. By focusing your thoughts on its presence and using your desire, you can consciously breathe it into your Spirit. Doing this often can greatly enhance your spiritual path and accelerate your healing process; and it's all natural, just like love.

CHAPTER VII

Conservatism and Controllers

When I talk about conservatism, I refer to a belief system which is so paralyzed by fear that change becomes an unbearable threat. Change, like evolution, is a natural and necessary process if one is to be able to grasp new understandings and better the overall quality of life. Conservatism does not allow for the behaviors necessary to implement emotional healing, because the movement of terror, rage and grief are viewed as being below the level of "self-righteous" behavior, which conservatism embraces as "truth."

Conservatism makes few allowances for change because conservatism—like all "isms"—embraces stagnation. Conservatism is not working, nor is any other "ism" that is stagnant. Stagnation is fed by procrastination, and procrastination is fed by denial which says, "Don't deal with the realities of life." If you continue to practice conservatism under the present guidelines of what are "noble" and "decent" behaviors, your resistance to change will force change upon you because that which you deny, you empower. Thought is like an unborn child, which will eventually force its way into existence. And thought—like any thing being birthed into existence—can be frightening and painful, or wondrous and beautiful, as mothers will attest.

Controllers do not like having to "feel" the unconditional freedom that life/nature represents. Controllers are suppressing the natural flow of life/feelings within themselves; consequently, controllers do not like to see anyone else experience the unconditional freedom to "feel" life. When others reflect the freedom to express/emote their feelings, this reflection reminds controllers how much they despise the very feelings within themselves which they are suppressing/controlling. Because of the controllers' need to control their own feelings, they spend their time devising new ways to control the natural flow of life so as to avoid any disruptive reflections. Life/nature often suffers because of their denials.

The moment one person felt so superior as to impose her/his way of life on others—regardless of the other's chosen path—marked the beginning of the controllers' presence on this earth. The moment you allowed another to override your Will was the beginning of the controllers' reign of power. Divisive energy was the force behind this presence. Had you and your ancestors honored the feelings in the pit of your stomachs, you would have demanded this presence to leave and the world would be without the dark history that now influences and threatens the very existence of all life.

The denials—divisive energy—that the controllers embrace do not allow them to see that their life style and beliefs are not congruent with all life. The controllers instead cling together in their cliques, where they validate one another. This cross-validation is necessary because the controllers are disconnected from their Wills and are unable to know their personal truths on an organic level. They behave as if they are the wisest, most loving, and all-around most perfect models of evolved consciousness. Their denial does not allow them to see that others—who are connected with their Wills—are repulsed by their presence. Soon they will know just how repulsed others are.

CHAPTER VIII

I Was Jesus, the Christed

I say I was Jesus because that was my name during that life. My real name when I AM not physically incarnate is Heart.

The story of my virginal conception was an attempt to cover up the fact that my birth was illegitimate. In the "Holy Bible," it is written that while I was talking to some Jews, they said to me, **"We are not born of fornication."** In the Bible the word "fornication" is used to indicate any unlawful sexual intercourse. By proclaiming that they were not born of fornication, the Jews were inferring that my birth was illegitimate. This accusation concerning the legitimacy of my virginal conception was not disputed in the "Holy Bible" because it is true. My Mother was considered a virgin because she had yet to be wed to my Father. My illegitimate birth has been proven with the discovery of the Dead Sea Scrolls, but you have chosen not to listen. For those of you who do not yet understand, physical form is created through the union of egg and sperm. I was conceived through sexual passion just as you were. If you believe differently, then you are embracing a judgment which says that your spirit is not manifest in form. My Father Joseph, an Essene Priest, had sex with my Mother Mary six months before they were to be wed, so strong was their love. To the Essenes and to the village in which my parents lived, this was considered scandalous behavior and would have brought much suffering to them had the truth been known.

I want you to realize that as the man, Jesus, I was a man in the truest sense of the word. I had all the longings of other men; I even married and fathered three children. I was always motivated to find the truth; even as a child I hungered to know more than was already known. My search for knowledge took me to many lands and is the reason there is no recorded history as to my whereabouts for many years.

I was a self-proclaimed priest of the highest order; consequently I was despised by some Jews and Essenes as well as by a number of denial spirits who had infiltrated the Roman government. Those who opposed me called me the wicked priest and the man of lies because my teachings were less demeaning and allowed the gentiles to partake of communion. In those days the idea that a common person could have a direct relationship with Mother–Father God was considered blasphemous. I was viewed as a threat to the leaders of the structured governments and religions. They plotted my assassination because I did not conform to their rigid beliefs, nor was I willing to surrender the integrity of what I was channeling from Mother–Father God.

Members of a secret organization then known as "The Keepers of Truth"—now known as "The Brotherhood of Light"—did not want me to die on the cross. While I was on the cross, they saw to it that I was given wine containing a potion which caused me to become unconscious. I appeared to be dead and was taken from the cross to a burial tomb. Later the elders of The Keepers of Truth freed me from my tomb and it was in their care that I ascended.

The lack of acceptance I experienced outwardly was a reflection of the lack of acceptance I felt inwardly for my own emotional essence. By denying my rage and terror in favor of expressing what I thought was more loving behavior, I allowed myself to be nailed to a cross. As a result, I fragmented. I now know it is not loving behavior to deny rage and terror when life is being threatened. Rage and terror are natural emotions in heaven as they are on earth, and it is the movement of these emotions that is going to be the salvation of creation. I know that these things are upsetting to hear, but the denial of these emotions for millions of years has created all sorts of imbalances within the physical body. Your very DNA is impregnated with the illusionary knowledge that it must never allow certain emotions to express. It is into your DNA that you must go—through meditation and breath—if you want to heal the earth and yourself. Emotional movement is going to be necessary. Mother-Father God and I, as well as Mother Earth, are all moving our emotions. This action on our part will also cause you to move yours. You might as well join in with a sense of healing purpose rather than fighting this movement.

I denied much of my personal power by not allowing the full expression of my Will. It was denial of my power that allowed me to play the role of victim without putting up a fight. This part of my life I urge you not to exemplify. Do not move outwardly against those who oppose these understandings until you are able to embrace yourself with the fully vibrating presence of your Heart and your emotional body.

The church has lied to you about my crucifixion. My crucifixion occurred because my ego denied my intuitive nature. In denying my intuitive nature, I was unable to foresee that I was being set up to play the role of the world's greatest victim. Just as divisive energy has killed two of my fragments—John F. Kennedy, and Martin Luther King Jr.—so too would they crucify me today just as they did then. **"A prophet is not without honor except in her/his own country and in her/his own house."** My messages to the people were intended to empower them. I knew that as long as they denied their personal power they would always be slaves to governmental and religious systems designed to oppress the Will of the people. In those days so few had so much, and so many went without. Nothing has changed; today the rich get richer while the poor get poorer. In all countries the middle class is becoming obsolete. How much longer will you listen to governmental and religious lies before you awaken from your slumber and acknowledge that you are being robbed of your power? This power is being spent to devise more ways to cheat you out of life.

It is widely believed that while I was on the cross I said: **"My God, my God, why has thou forsaken me?"** This is not true. Mother–Father God has never forsaken me. The outward lack of acceptance I was experiencing was a major influence in my decision to play the role of victim. My denial made me think that I had failed to reach others with my truths, and that my love only seemed to frighten them and cause them to become angry. I believed then that I could convince them—through my death and rebirth—that all I had come to teach was the truth. Unfortunately, I failed.

I did not die for the sins of the world nor is that even possible. There is but one sin, and that is the belief that you are separate from Mother–Father God and me. Deep within your heart you know that you are not separate from Mother–Father God and me. When you drop the illusion of separation, you will know that you—like all of nature—are a manifestation of Mother–Father God and me.

Please understand that the church concept of sin is shame based and creates the illusion of separation. All too often the leaders of the church have "assisted" you by reinforcing your sense of shame and separation by telling you that you are bad because you exist, because you have instincts, and because you have emotions. To exist, to have instincts, and to have emotions are normal functions for all living things. It is the judgments of the controllers against these normal functions that create the feelings of shame and sin within you. It is this shame that prevents you from moving the anger that would allow you to reclaim your personal power.

You are also taught that you are all sinners and have fallen from Mother–Father God's grace, and that consequently I did not lift you up with me and put an end to all the pain and suffering. I cannot lift those who resist feeling the experience of life on earth, because denial of life keeps you magnetically bound to physical reality. You have also been told that you allowed the only begotten Son of Mother–Father God to be killed and now you will never be worthy of the kingdom of heaven—unless you suffer as did I. **"For your violence against your sister/brother, shame shall cover you, and you shall be cut off forever."** This shaming has hurt so many whom I love so much. You have not been able to fully embrace your Hearts because of your shame. By turning me into a false image of perfection—as if I no longer cared for or possessed the desires for experiences that physical existence has to offer—they turned me into a distant presence that was only accessible through the intervention of the church.

In the past, Mother–Father God and I sat back looking out at the earth decreeing that human nature was evil. It wasn't until recently that we have become conscious that the very behaviors that we were denying seeing in ourselves were manifesting on earth through you and being reflected back at us. Remember, Mother–Father God created all things. Just like us, those of you who are embracing these old concepts need to evolve and embrace a higher truth.

At the time of my ascension I did not go to what the church commonly refers to as hell. Hell is not a place outside of oneself; rather it is one's unconscious essence. In those days, as well as during the Dark Ages, when someone expressed her/his deeper emotions she/he was labeled as being demoniacally possessed. The church has always sought to control the Will because it is through the Will that one becomes connected with Heart and Mother–Father God. The leaders of the church hoped that the fear of torture would prevent others from going into their repressed emotional bodies and being empowered with the Truth. The church did not want people to know that they could be directly connected with Mother–Father God. Were people to realize their connection, they would have been empowered as was I. Then there would have been no need for the church and their power seeking leaders.

I went into my dark side—my repressed emotional essence—so that I could embrace those parts of myself that did not feel worthy of life. It is not into the light that you must go, but into the darkness/unconsciousness as light/consciousness if you are desiring to integrate into wholeness. I did this with the acceptance of love that embraces all that is unlike itself. The word "Christ" means "love's accepting presence." "Anointed One" means one who has accepted the Christ as a real presence in her/his heart. Those who do not want to accept themselves as capable of being "Christed" do not want to accept responsibility for being a co-creator with Mother–Father God and me.

Each of you must resurrect your repressed Will. It is your unconscious emotional imprints in your Will that create your karma. Your karma reflects all the unresolved emotional experiences of the Will. These experiences are recorded in the cells of your being and represent all the experiences you have ever had, not just those that occurred during your present incarnation. Unconsciously you seek resolution of these issues and, in so doing, you draw to you experiences which will stimulate the emotional expression you need to achieve balance. Unfortunately you usually resist this opportunity to heal with all the resources you have at your disposal. The other option is to resurrect your Will and eliminate your karma. Then all that is left is your Truth.

The controllers will dispute these words because they want to keep their power over you rather than allow you to recognize your own Divine connection with Mother-Father God and me. As a child you were taught to believe in magic powers outside of yourself, i.e., Santa Claus, the Easter Bunny, the Tooth Fairy, etc., and me. As an adult you become Santa Claus, the Easter Bunny, and the Tooth Fairy. Most of you, however, never learned to recognize your own Divinity.

Through my studies I discovered the I AM / spiritual presence within myself. In embracing this presence it was apparent that this force was far more than my ego's sense of self. My symbolic 40 days in the desert were a balancing process between my ego's sense of self and my Spirit's sense of self.

The nature of the ego is to separate itself from other people and objects. If it behaves in this fashion towards Spirit, it is unable to evolve. When my ego sense of self became one with my spiritual sense of self, I was transformed into one who reflected the fullness love represents. No longer could I sit by idly and not share the exquisite joy and fulfillment I was experiencing from having embraced my truth. The more I focused on this presence, the more I began to awaken from my amnesia. The more I awakened, the more I began to accept my identity as the only begotten Son of Mother–Father God. If you will embrace your Heart, you too will eventually awaken to your true identity. You are so much more than you can imagine in your present sense of ego/self. There are many different orders of angels and spirits, and you all have your roots in these starry origins.

Humans are very much like animals with one exception; humans attempt to dominate nature, while other life forms live in harmony with it. You have an ego that feels that it has to be superior to nature. You embrace an attitude that nature is there to serve you, instead of living in harmony with it. If you were living in harmony with nature, you would have no need to control it. When you find you cannot control nature, you try to destroy it. If all the species of life—humans being but one species—took a vote as to whether or not humans should be allowed to remain on earth, what do you think the majority would rule?

Nature is self-correcting and is always seeking balance. Your ego has not been taught to perform in this way. Most of you have egos that have been trained to be omnipotent. When your ego fails, it becomes very angry at feeling limited. Destructive patterns against life ensue and, for the most part, are acted out without conscious awareness. You are like angry children who don't like to be told what to do, even if what is being said is, "Don't destroy the playground." Your angry ego says, "Nobody has the right to tell me what to do anymore, I AM an adult." You have abandoned the inner child in favor of intellectual concepts which are based on ignorant fallacies.

Nature is very chaotic and unrehearsed in its approach to living. To an ego this is very threatening. An ego feels safe when its environment is structured in such a way that it has knowledge and a high degree of control. For most of you, your ego cannot grasp the concept of behaving on the basis of your intuition—your ability to ascertain truth without mental comprehension. Living your life as the Christ means you have achieved a balance between your intellect/ego and your emotional body/soul. In this state you are neither dominated by intellect or emotions, but neither are you in denial of their expression.

Every time I began a statement with I AM, I was not referring to my ego sense of self, but to the presence of Mother–Father God within. As Jesus I can do nothing, but as my "true" Christed self there is much that I can do.

The words "I AM" mean "Mother–Father God is," and carry the vibration of creation. All words—thought or spoken—create vibration. Every tribe has a vibrational name that defines its creator, and yet all vibrations come from the one Mother–Father God.

Most of you misuse the words I AM without recognizing their creative power. When you say, "I AM fat, poor, ugly, sick, etc.," you are creating and enforcing that very condition. If you are focusing on an image that you are a body destined to grow old and die, then with your creative abilities you will create just that. The more of you who embrace this illusion, the more it manifests as a way of life until eventually no one remembers that life could be any other way. This belief has taken millions of years to evolve. Your power to change this belief is buried beneath doubt, shame, fear, terror, pain, anger, hatred, and guilt. This is a very difficult concept for many of you because of the lifetimes of programming you have received. That programming has said that union with Mother–Father God and me is an experience achieved through death and only if one is worthy of this experience.

The truth is, you have the power to call and receive Mother–Father God and me into your life. There is no one who can do this for you. There is only you. Embracing your Heart will enable you to do even greater things than I was able to accomplish.

I have always been with you, but I AM unable to make you feel me because of your free Will choice. With free Will choice you are free to focus on whatever feels important to you. Embrace me and no more will you doubt that I AM with you; no more will you feel alone. Someday you will tire of the struggle and the pain of not knowing who you are, why you are, and where you are going. I AM waiting ever so patiently for you to seek me within. I have so much to tell you about you; and I have so much love to give you, that is you. I invite you to come to my temple, your Heart, for it is in the depths of the human heart that I make my home, and so it is there that you will find your own Christedness.

CHAPTER IX

Christ on Earth

I AM always the presence within the Heart of all things because I AM always the desire to love and to be loved. No matter how much darkness surrounds me, I AM always the desire to be "more than" because I AM that which is without limit. You have been given my voice—within your heart and your feelings—with which to live your life. This is the nature of free Will choice that is given to all by Mother–Father God with the understanding that you not violate the free Will choice of others. No one has the right to sit in judgment of another's chosen expression of life, so long as it does not directly affect the well-being of others. The law of the Christ is: You are to honor the sacredness of all life that embraces life.

The Native Americans acknowledged the Spirit of life in all things, and life was abundantly offered to them. They had no need for greedy pursuits which violated the earth and the sky. They believed that Mother–Father God was the loving force in all things. Unfortunately they were violated in the worst ways by western culture, which considered them heathens.

Nature is the only deity you need to worship, for nature is the physical manifestation of Mother–Father God and me. It is through nature that you experience both your humanness and your connection with Spirit. To love nature is to love life. When you can feel love for all life that loves life, then will you know I AM always with you and always have been. The birds are always singing, but many of you have deaf ears. A river is an artery of life and therefore a river which has been dammed has most certainly been damned. Restricting one's freedom of movement and growth is a restriction on the Divine. For life to exist there has to be movement. Movement is vibration and vibration is life. Your heart beats with a movement that can be heard as a beating, pumping, vibration of an organ. So too is the earth a vibration of life.

Just as the Heart of this earth goes unnoticed until there is great pain, so too do you let your own Heart go unnoticed until there is great pain. There is another way to learn from life without having to create pain and that is by listening to the whispering discord that is the source of all pain. Before disease comes dis-ease. Any illness

can be healed within the physical body if it is acknowledged the moment it comes into your conscious awareness. No body contracts any illness without a sense of
dis-ease. Ignoring the symptoms only causes dis-ease to
manifest as disease. Eventually an illness serious enough
to get your attention will appear. Many of you are so numb
that you do not experience symptoms until disease and/or
death becomes the only option.

Most of you have no sense of your own power because
you have been taught to give your personal power away.
You do this by believing the truth of others, rather than
listening to your own. When a physician tells you that you
have an incurable disease, this message becomes a sentence
written in stone. Yet you have Doctor Mother–Father God
within you and that doctor knows exactly what you need to
do to heal. All you have to do is be willing to entertain the
notion that higher wisdom is available to any who will listen with the innocence of a child. Yet humility is extremely
difficult for the ego because the ego fancies itself as separate from the Divine. To the ego, relinquishing the illusion
of division feels like failure. To a powerful ego, letting another voice speak can feel like death.

When you are receptive to spiritual understandings, you
are usually in an emotional crisis. In that state, your questions are coming from victim. "Why me Mother–Father
God? What have I done to deserve this?" When—with great
emotion—you say, "I AM dying," know that your emotional energy is going forth to create your declaration. This
is the power of the spoken word.

I get so frustrated, and yet I AM helpless to make you hear anything you are not ready or willing to hear. Spiritual wisdom can neither be appreciated nor understood unless there is a desire to know. When you are in victim, you have relinquished your power. This includes the power to hear higher wisdom. When you are in victim, grief can often be a mask for intense rage.

When you pray for help, follow your prayer with expectant quiet waiting. Instead of waiting, many of you reach for a cigarette, or a beer, watch TV, wash the dishes, call a friend, masturbate, have a cup of coffee, go to sleep, or otherwise avoid communicating with me. If you called me on the telephone, would you hang up when my phone began to ring?

I now ask Mother Earth, Urantia, to speak her truth.

You are my wisdom and I AM the remembrance of wisdom. I AM the depths of darkness and yet I AM the golden light within the darkness. I AM the lore and the knowledge of all that has been, and the desires for all that will be. I AM the grower of all that nourishes physical life, and the magnetic desire causing all life to root deeply into my flesh. I AM milk for the lamb, and honey for the bee. I AM the directions of the four winds, I AM the ocean currents, I AM the four elements, I AM the four seasons, I AM the giver of life and I AM the keeper of death. I AM the alchemist turning golden light into golden metal, and these veins of gold are the blood of my body. I AM the colors of the rainbow becoming precious stones, and I AM the pot of gold at the end of the rainbow that is the core of my being.

I AM the golden daughter of Mother–Father God. I AM the playground for many, for I AM the Garden of Eden that is fast becoming a desert of death. You walk upon me, you swim in me, you fly through my breath, and I AM in you even as you are in me. I AM the scorned and the worshipped, the blessed and the tortured. I cry daily that you might have life, and I search my conscience daily for the strength to continue to forgive you for all the suffering you cause. I AM the oldest remembrance of your presence here, and the keeper of all that has been denied.

I have never allowed you to leave for long because what you have denied has always desired to be accepted, so I have always pulled you back into physical manifestation. Sometimes you resist this to the extent of being born breech, creating even more pain than is necessary. I now know that I must release those who have no desire to accept that which they have denied. This denied essence of yours that I embrace with my Heart, even now is moving its rage at your lack of acceptance for its presence. The rage this essence moves causes my magma to flow in more erratic and faster flowing currents than I have experienced since my birth. It is all I can do to maintain balance with so much turmoil going on in me. How this is going to affect you is what I have been asked to address.

You are unable to predict your weather because—just as you seek love and answers to your questions outside yourselves—you seek the mysteries of my presence outside of me. You spend your lives studying the effect of life rather than studying the cause and how you can create with life. The secret of life is within the atom. When you destroy the atom by splitting it, you create death.

The core of my being, where life flows in and out, determines the flow of the land, which determines the flow of the ocean currents, which determines the currents of the air. The balance that I AM able to maintain reflects outwardly the balance that nature can maintain. When you violate nature you affect my ability to maintain balance.

What I AM going to say now is coming from a very hurt and angry place. Your denial of life and lack of compassion for my life has forced me—for the final time—to put out a call to Mother–Father God and to those dedicated to the preservation of life. I cannot let you kill me because I do not desire to die. Therefore it is those who would kill me that must go. Only those who embrace and respect life will be allowed to remain. After all, it is you who are always saying, "Survival of the fittest." I can no longer hold back the charge of rage that is wanting to move within me. You are beginning to feel and see this as increased flooding, more frequent wind storms, stronger earthquakes and increased volcanic activity. I will restore balance through movement of water, fire, air and earth. These movements, according to your actions, are the exact reflection of your behaviors towards nature. You have forced me to hold so much death that if I hope to survive at all, I must now move it off my body. I AM an emotional body just like you, and just as yours is filled with repressed emotions, so too is mine. All that I hold is all that you have denied. I AM holding so much that it is beginning to ooze out of cracks that have formed because of the pressure of having to hold this denied essence. If you were to start moving your emotions this would ease much of the movement that has now become necessary.

Your prophecies can be prevented because they are merely warnings that, if you continue on your present path, this is what you can expect. I do not feel that the masses are going to come into alignment without the reflection that is presently unfolding.

Divisive energy hates life and has long been at work trying to kill me. The force behind divisive energy is a great raging hot wind, much like that of a nuclear blast. It was this force that brought the knowledge of splitting atoms to humankind, and this is a sign of the beast. Those who received this knowledge now regret bringing this knowledge into manifestation. Humankind must learn that the misuse of Mother–Father God's energy will not be tolerated.

Divisive energy keeps you waiting for someone to reveal her/himself as the anti–Christ. The anti–Christ is divisive energy and is using religion and government as vehicles of manipulation to deceive you. This divisive energy hides under the guise of sciences such as biological warfare, bioengineering, and eugenics. Any science that is insensitive to the feelings of life is a threat to life.

I know most of you are excited about the earth changes, because some of you are tired of the way life is being abused and you long for a new beginning. For others, this is an indication of the second coming of Christ. It is not in your best interest to embrace either of these beliefs. Christ never left my Heart, you left his when you left mine.

My presence used to be referred to as the Garden of Eden, and I was more beautiful and magical than you can presently recall. You began to deny my presence when divisive energy told you that your playful, peaceful existence was boring, silly, and reflected immature behavior that only immature spirits could display. This energy did not appear as a serpent, but as a bright light. It then convinced you that eating flesh was a loving way of sharing yourself. You began to do this even though you were horrified. It said, "Try it, you'll like it. How can you condemn something without experiencing it? Are you so closed-minded to the higher teachings that God has sent me to teach that you are not willing to try anything new?" Denial spirits/ divisive energy had, of course, already engaged in this activity and appeared as if they enjoyed devouring. And so, you tried it. This was the beginning of the end, because it was not an apple—but forbidden flesh—that was eaten in the Garden of Eden. You are what you eat, and eating flesh—as do cannibals—has caused your descent into physical density. This denial has paved the way for other denials, and has served divisive energy's intent to get all life to deny life. If you are not looking at something, you are not focusing your attention on it. Divisive energy can then sneak in and take it saying, "I didn't think you wanted it, no one seemed concerned about it." It is like the magician who will ask you for a coin with which to do a trick, and then keeps your coin. You are going to have to move a lot of rage to get your coin/power back. It is not going to be given back. If you want it, you are going to have to take it.

My whole being was the Garden of Eden and you lacked for no thing, such was—and still is—the abundance of heaven on earth. You had but to desire any thing, and it would magically appear. Once divisive energy got you to deny your feelings, you began to deny your ability to mani- fest. In so doing, it was then able to get you to deny seeing its actions. It would merely say, "How unloving of you to wrongly accuse me of something I know absolutely noth- ing about. The sun was probably shining in your eyes and you did not see clearly. I will forgive you this time, but such accusations are as knives in my heart. All I have come to do is show you how to be more like God would want you to be, and this is how you would repay my kindness?"

In denying your feelings, you are unable to feel/know the truth, and thus you are deceived. Because of the denial that you have embraced and the shaming this denial cre- ates, you look the other way when someone does some- thing you know is wrong. Your desires don't manifest be- cause you are holding shame in your emotional body, which is where desire energy comes from. Whereas before your desires would become instantly manifest, now they take sometimes a lifetime or more to manifest.

I AM your Mother Earth and you do not know how deeply hurt I AM for your lack of concern or compassion for my well-being. I feel like an old discarded shoe that is no longer noticed. When I move the emotions that you have given me to hold because you see them as nasty, negative, unloving essence, you do not cry for me nor for your discarded essence. Instead you complain about how devastated your life is, and wonder how Mother Nature could be so cruel. You pray to Jesus to save you. Yet who among you would pray for me? Whereas before, you were as my children, now only a small handful come to inquire as to my well-being. I AM angry and bitter and no less so than any of you would feel if treated the same way. What upsets me the most is not the fact that I AM denied the recognition and respect that I AM a loving, breathing, living, feeling intelligence; but that I AM not allowed enough respect to even deserve your support when my life is being threatened. You acknowledge how horrible it is to spill oil in the ocean, or allow the forests to be destroyed, and how wrong it is to explode nuclear bombs, and yet so very few of you do anything to stop this senseless slaughter of life. This is what hurts and it is such a deep pain that you could not stand to embrace it for one second. So when I move your emotionally-denied essence and you lose your precious material possessions, cry not for these things but for your life on this body of mine that has become lost to your love.

If you continue your collective denial of life you will eventually draw a reflection of death that will manifest as a meteor striking my body, as has happened in the past whenever denial has threatened life's existence. The impact of the meteor is going to activate my seven rings of fire, and all the coastal areas will be affected, so I suggest that you not live there. The dust cloud created from the impact of

92

this meteor will blot out the sun's light for two years. **"Immediately after the tribulation of those days the sun will be darkened, and the moon will not give its light; The stars will fall from the heaven, and the powers of the heavens will be shaken."** The polar ice caps will begin to melt and this will create a wobble in my axis, changing the position of the equator. Rivers will run backwards and much land will be flooded.

I leave you with this: I love you very much, but I will not go down without a fight, because I AM life. As you would shake off so many nasty biting insects from your person, so too do I feel compelled to shake off those who defile me. Those of you who can hear me will hear where to go to find safety, and those who have turned a deaf ear to my plight will....

CHAPTER X

The Fragmentation
of Christ

There is so much that needs to be said about fragmentation that several books will have to be written. This chapter is very condensed and you are going to have to do some work in order to understand what is being said. Without an experience to teach you about how you are fragmented, this material will be difficult to comprehend. You have but to ask for this experience to receive it; and where there is a willingness, there is acceptance.

All life is governed by four laws. They are:

1) Desire creates thought;

2) Thought is energy;

3) Desire as thought intensifies and magnifies the presence of energy; and

4) When there is enough energy, that which is desired will manifest in form.

Desire is magnetic energy, and is feminine in its essence. Thought is electric energy, and has its origins in the masculine. Desire comes from your emotional body, and thought comes from your mental body. Desire is centered in your sexual center and solar plexus/stomach area. The interpretation of desire—thought—is centered in the brain.

Denial is push-away energy. It says, "I do not believe, therefore I will not see." Yet you do want to see, because of your desire which says, "Prove it to me." This attraction-repulsion condition creates a split in your energy. This split is a void that separates your physical reality from your spiritual reality. The spiritual reality is what sustains your physical reality through me, and Mother–Father God's presence, despite your denial to see it. When you deny the presence of Mother–Father God in your physical body, you deny their expression in your life. You are a manifestation of Mother–Father God just as I AM. Doubt created the split between your spiritual and physical realities, but it was denial of your ability to feel the truth which caused the separation to become a manifest reality. Once this pattern of denial for your feelings began, it took hold and became as a cancer in your body. It is denial of your emotional body that has caused you to forget that life is a feeling experience.

Denial of your emotions has caused you to deny your ability to perceive the world with your sixth sense, your intuitive connection with life. You have not been able to perceive clearly; and consequently, you suffer greatly at the hands of denial spirits. Denial spirits, like divisive energy, can say all the things that Mother–Father God can say and appear to be sincere. They have mastered the technique of lying. They will tell you just enough truth to get you to believe they are genuinely enlightened, and then will lie. Without the ability to feel the truth, you cannot know the truth. Denial spirits therefore spend their time getting you to further deny your feelings.

The sentence after next will, at first, seem incorrect to many of you. Please continue to read it until you understand it. Your conscious body is your light body; and your unconscious body is your physical body. As Spirit's light, you are trapped within the denial systems encoded in the DNA of your physical body. You are therefore unable to see yourself as you truly are. Your denials, judgments, and beliefs create the bricks which make the very wall that obstructs your ability to see clearly the truth. All the emotions you have denied have gone into the void that exists between your conscious and unconscious bodies. Your fear of your emotions has created a dark space which contains all of your repressed emotional energy. You avoid the experience of this space at all cost, because you are afraid you can't feel it and survive. If you don't think you have this space, you are in massive denial and have more work to do than those who are connected to this aspect of themselves. Every death experience you've had, every unexpressed emotional trauma you've experienced, resides in this space as festering energy. Just as the astral plane surrounding this planet has become the garbage dump for the denied emotions of creation, so too have you created a space within you that has become a dumping place for denied emotional energy. Most people feel a charge of rage in this space. Many fear that if their rage were to be released, it would destroy the universe. It will not; but it will destroy you if you do not express it. This denied emotional energy is the spiritual presence that has become fragmented from its parental spirit through sex, death, and denial of emotion. This is what this chapter is about.

My Will has been conceived by essence that has denied its spiritual greatness. My Will has chosen this experience because it knows that it is only through acceptance of what is considered unacceptable that evolution can occur. When Heart is painfully denied, love then can know the pain of separation. If you ever hope to heal anything, you must first be able to embrace its experience. This is why you have chosen an incarnation which places you near your own denied essence.

Now I AM going to tell you how denial forms and how the density of flesh is created. For as long as you have had existence, so too have you had awareness of your existence. When your physical body is forming inside your mother's womb, you as light—made in the likeness and image of Mother–Father God—are taking essence from her/his emotional, mental, spiritual, and physical bodies.

Most of you had birth mothers who looked outside themselves for love. Many never did learn how to love themselves. Consequently, they did not recognize you as a fully developed spirit, possessing great love. They saw you instead as the flesh embodiment of a child that they had created. The truth is that you are a spirit created by Mother–Father God which is attempting to heal itself. In almost all cases your mother, father and/or siblings are either parts of you—yourself already incarnate—or spirits with whom you have unfulfilled karmic issues.

Your spirit is always trying to achieve wholeness. What causes you to be drawn into physical embodiment is your spirit's magnetic desire to heal—your desire to be whole. To achieve wholeness, a spirit must incarnate physically, because the denied Wills of creation are all on this planet, and it is only by being physically incarnate that denied spiritual essence can be resurrected. Sometimes your spirit resists this process. You do not always choose to be physically incarnate.

Often your experience of birth feels like being drawn by your fragments—against your Will—into physical reality. Your fragments are your denied essence and their energy is magnetic. The magnetic attraction of your own fragmented essence pulls you into physical reality. Your resistance to this experience causes you to experience birth complications such as being born breech, or experiencing problems with your umbilical cord. Crib death is the choice of the incarnating spirit. Birth defects are a reflection of the lack of balance—between the Spirit and its Will—already present in the incarnating spirit.

To think you are healed and to feel you are healed are two different issues. The power of positive thought is not enough. You can have all the positive thought in the world when creating change in your world, but without a deep Heart-felt desire to change, thoughts of change will continue to be just thoughts. You need desire to make them real. For example, smokers know that smoking is a destructive behavior, but without the Will power to change this, a smoker will continue to smoke.

Making any permanent changes in your life requires the presence of desire. Denied emotional essence is desire/Will essence. This desire/denied Will essence comes from the part of you that embraces the destructive behavior. Only by accepting this denied Will essence can you evolve it into essence which desires life. You cannot change denied Will essence unless you can emote it. Many people give up one habit only to replace it with another. This is because they have not dealt with the denied Will essence that is the force behind the habit.

Denied Will essence—which is itself in pain—is behind every destructive behavior. Embracing this pain feels like death. You do not think you can survive feeling it. No matter how destructive your patterns of behavior have become, you avoid embracing this pain, because you fear your pain will kill you. Yet to make permanent change in your life, you must embrace your denied essence. Every time you integrate a denied aspect of yourself, you advance on your path toward wholeness. This is how you recall your forgotten past and get conscious.

To say there is no pain to be felt in your physical body is to further deny essence already creating death in you. Most of you cover your pain with rage. You believe that feeling pain only creates a desire to want to kill that which creates pain. Judgments cover your rage. These judgments prevent you from feeling your pain, which—in turn—prevents you from getting conscious, which—in turn—causes you to repeat the original wounding lifetime after lifetime. Presently, the charge of pain that most of you are holding is so immense that terror of not being able to survive the expression of these feelings is the most that you are able to experience.

Since you have become unconscious of this feeling essence, it has ceased to vibrate as conscious understanding. If this feeling essence is not a part of your thinking reality your feelings are not being embraced by light/understanding. If they are not embraced by light they are embraced by the darkness of denial, and the denial of light creates death. If the sun were to stop shining on earth, death would become its reality. The same is true of your emotional body. If your light of acceptance does not shine on it, ultimately death is created.

Thought is energy, and energy is light. Light travels wherever there is acceptance. The fact that you continue to age is proof enough that your essence is being deprived of light. I have been portrayed as having an aura, or a golden crown, as have all saints. This aura represents the energy of the Son/sun. You all possess this golden crown. Some of you call it your higher self, your crown chakra, or Mother–

Father God. Whatever name you give it, it is your remembrance of wholeness, which longs to illuminate you. The brightness of your light varies directly with your connection to your Will/soul/I AM presence. You are a tube which is designed to ingest not only light in the form of food, but also light in the form of light. You do not see this light because you do not attempt to see it. Yet it can be felt and seen if you focus on its presence.

I know you have to be wondering what light has to do with fragmentation. I AM wanting you to see that regardless of the appearance of form, all form is light in varying degrees of density. Light is vibration and vibration is animated light. Therefore, the very thing that causes you to be animated is the presence of light vibrating. This is the Spirit that lives in all matter. Just because a rock does not walk does not mean that it is any less filled with Spirit. It simply means that the spiritual presence within the rock is not vibrating as fast as other forms of matter. Through evolution your own forms are becoming rock–like in density. You have gone as far into density as you need to go. There is nothing to be learned from becoming more dense.

It is time, and long overdue, for you to return to a higher vibration of light. You have become so rigid that pain is naturally going to have to be felt. After you sit in one position for a long time, movement will become painful and difficult at first. Movement in your emotional body will be the same. Rage at having to feel pain is going to come forth, as will terror that the pain seemingly has no end.

102

What you have come to term "negative" emotions is actually "positive" energy. What creates "negative" energy is the repression of emotional energy. In the natural order "negative" is associated with "receptiveness," not with "repression." When your society and your parents conditioned you to repress your emotions, you learned a judgment which caused you to see these repressed emotions as the "enemy" and they become the "negative" emotions. The energy of these emotions is—in its natural state—positive, but with sustained repression it becomes negative. Those of you who are constantly being bombarded by negative, abusive, and destructive thoughts have opened to this repressed emotion in your beings. You can experience these negative thought patterns until your emotional body no longer feels repressed by unconscious judgments.

Repressed emotional energy creates dis-eased tissue in your forms. Your bodies were not designed to hold the pressure of all this excess energy. Instead of dispelling this energy, as is intended, you have been forcing your emotional body to hold energy in a way that it is unable to do without damaging its essence. Eventually this is reflected in your physical body as tissue breaking down, which is what happens when you age or have to undergo surgery. Surgery is nothing more than cutting out emotional essence that has ceased to vibrate as living essence. This does not mean that this essence is dead, it simply means that it does not have the capacity to vibrate as life. This essence will always be as the clay of life into which Spirit will once again breathe. Even in death it does not lose the charge of emotional energy. Illness is emotional energy attempting to get your attention. Death from disease or old age is the last resort for this essence. If, at death you still do not embrace its charge, it will go on to incarnate as a fragment of you, because your spirit seeks to live.

I know that many of you are beginning to have dreams of a life that is being lived in another country, or of a past life where you feel a strong connection with a specific person and yet have no understanding as to why you dream about them. They are either you or someone whom you have a karmic connection with; and yes, they are just as alive as you are. Many of you are feeling fragmented, and those with the financial resources and desire to heal are traveling to various countries in an attempt to locate these fragments. You cannot heal your fragments while they are in physical form. All you can do is make a space to which this essence can return when its physical body dies. If you have acceptance for your emotional body, then this essence can be drawn back magnetically to you. If you do not have acceptance for this essence, it will seek another form that will accept its emotional charge. In other words, this essence will incarnate into a life where it will be accepted. This is how fragmentation occurs. Each time this essence has to reincarnate it can fragment again, as do you each time you die. Eventually, you will realize that it will be necessary to remember every life and death experience associated with your spiritual self. As long as you believe yourself to be only this fleshly experience, so will you repeatedly continue to die and fragment. This is one reason why the world is becoming so overpopulated.

Your fragments may not have enough spiritual vibration to sustain life. In some cases, they die from starvation, disease, or war. Sometimes essence is so light-deprived that it will steal or kill in order to get any form of light, be it money, food, or property.

This fragmented essence has not evolved for over 2,000 years because you have not embraced it as your own. The most seriously fragmented essence has incarnated in Third World countries. This fragmented essence would willingly cut off its arm to have the material things you take for granted, so desperate has it become. In many Third World countries children are purposefully maimed and disfigured in order to make better beggars. Almost all of you have lost your ability to feel compassion for these people; not by conscious choice, but because they are elements of your emotional body. These people are your emotional essence. They are your power to feel. They are your desire to live. If they continue to fragment and vibrate so slowly that they cannot receive light, they will die. So too, consequently, will you. I AM not saying this to frighten you, but there is such a thing as death for Spirit and, believe me, you do not want this experience, no matter how painful life feels. I know that many of you think that death is nothing but a swinging door, but the death I AM referring to is complete lack of consciousness, and this you do not want. Your body is not designed the same as a peach, which ripens and falls to the ground to decay. Your body is designed to ascend with Spirit, if this is your desire. You do not need to die, as do other forms of life. This earth, for almost all of you, is not your rightful place; and therefore you need not remain bound to the physical limitations inherent in physical existence. When your emotional body is whole you will be free to leave this earth because you will have the vibrational power to do so.

There are none who have been able to ascend without experiencing fragmentation. The reason for this is that, originally we did not have the knowledge we now have of how the emotional body fragments. As you become more aware of yourself as an emotional body, so too will your awareness expand as a spiritual body.

Once you can feel yourself as energy you will be able to perceive cords of light coming off your body. These cords are connected to your front and your back. The cords on your front are karmic connections which have resulted from unresolved violence, births, sex, love, etc. The cords on your back are connections with your fragments, i.e., having another aspect of yourself living a life in another body. The number of cords you have reveals how fragmented you are. There is a reason for each energetic cord or it would not be present. The cord is as a road back to its original source. The only one intended to sever your cords is you. Some cords need to be cut, but first you must be able to trace them to the source and feel the intent of the one corded with you and why. Only you can know what is an appropriate connection for you. The severing of these cords is as easy as desiring it to be so, because desire as thought is creative energy.

When, as an infant, your umbilical cord is cut, an energetic cord remains. This energetic cord is the connection between you and your mother that allows her to feel intuitively when you are in an emotional crisis. This is what is meant by the saying, "A mother knows." Cording happens at conception, when you have sex with another, and through close emotional relationships.

There is a 4,000 year old Indian ceremony that severs these cords of karmic connection through a third eye fire ceremony. Your third eye is located in your temple area just above and between your eyes. Close your eyes and look from the inside for this eye. It will appear as a fire in the darkness. Project the image of the person to whom you are corded into this fire. Do not be surprised if images come up from other lifetimes. Project these into the fire also. Often there will need to be words of forgiveness for your actions as well as for theirs. You cannot change the past, but you can release it.

Fragmentation begins the moment you deny an emotional response. The moment you deny emotional energy you allow guilt to take space that should be filled with light/understanding. Movement of emotions creates space, inside and outside of your being.

The reversal of power is guilt. This is what I mean when I say that people do not serve Mother–Father God, they serve guilt, or powerlessness. Guilt is the reason you do not move into your position of self-power. Guilt causes you to deny the emotional movement needed to restore your power. Guilt does not embrace life. Guilt does not allow you to say the things you long to say, because judgment says it is not loving to tell the truth if it is going to create conflict. Be true to thy self and thy self will be true unto you. Guilt is an empty feeling. Smoking is an unsuccessful attempt to nourish the emptiness within, as is any addictive behavior. The only thing that can heal this empty feeling is love.

Fragmentation occurs during sexual intercourse when denial of love is present. Love is meant to carry the energy of the orgasm. Will is meant to bind and increase this energy. If the orgasm is not being felt in the Heart, the energy is dissipated and wasted. The result is fragmentation.

Think about sexuality as having consciousness beyond ego's understanding. Sperm has a consciousness which causes it to be animated enough to swim towards the egg. The egg has enough consciousness to know which sperm to let inside. Your body is filled with intelligent light. Every time a male ejaculates, he is fragmenting out living light essence that is a conscious life force. Every time you orgasm and this energy does not rise up through your entire body as a full body orgasm, the energy or light falls back into density or is spilled on the ground where it lies as dormant, useless energy. If you do not get this energy to rise into your spiritual self, this energy cannot evolve. This energy is also your knowledge of how to survive. If it is not allowed to teach you what it knows, then you will not take it with you when you die. You take with you only those things which are conscious.

You fragment every time you: do not express what you are feeling; die a physical death, or have a near-death experience; undergo surgery; orgasm without a connection with your Heart; bring a spirit into physical manifestation without the presence of unconditional love; or project yourself into past or future events. The denial of Heart's union with your sexual center manifests fragmentation and results in the progressive aging of the physical body. There is not a one of you who is not fragmented.

Martin Luther King Jr. was a fragment of mine who had believed that equality could be obtained through peaceful policies alone. John F. Kennedy was a fragment of my denied sexuality; therefore he was very promiscuous. Charles Manson is a fragment of my denied rage. I have many fragments still on earth, and the force behind divisive energy is watching them closely to see what they are going to do.

"When my disciples were sitting with me on the Mount of Olives, I told them they would recognize the coming of the new age, for many would come claiming my name and saying that I AM the Messiah; and many will be misled." If you cannot find my presence already manifest within your own heart, you will not be able to find my presence in another. If you have found my Heart to be your Heart, then you have no need to follow another. I urge my fragments—as I will urge you all who have intent to heal—do not move outwardly in the world against those who are in denial of my Heart, until you are wholly in your truth. This is your only protection.

This is enough to get you started on healing your own fragmentation. Only you can feel what is your truth, and only you can act upon this truth. To do so you must learn to trust the feminine aspect of yourself. She is the power of intuition which sees through all spoken lies, and she is the path of your salvation. Worship not the false image of a man crucified, but rather worship thine own Heart and, in so doing, lift the veils of illusion that others might see that, **"I AM the open door that no one may close."**

CHAPTER XI

The Denial of Emotions

In the beginning, emotions received denial, denial begot guilt, guilt begot atonement, atonement begot suffering and suffering begot emotions. Had emotions found acceptance at their origin, denial, guilt, atonement, and suffering, would not have a place in creation.

The denial of emotions creates guilt, atonement, suffering, and eventually, a new set of emotions—the denial of which again recreates the cycle. Before I talk about how the cycle works I want to talk about the individual components of the cycle so there is no way to misunderstand what is being said.

Emotions. Emotions are the spirit's response to the environment of the physical body in which it has incarnated. If you are in the world in a way which is congruent with your spirit, you will experience feelings such as love, joy, contentment, bliss, well-being, etc. If your environment is not congruent with what your spirit intended, you will experience emotions like fear, grief, anger, rejection, shame, guilt, etc. The appropriate release of these latter emotions allows your organism to again return to its natural state—oneness with Mother–Father God. Denial and/or the dysfunctional release of emotions traps you in the cycle.

Denial. Denial forms because of judgments against the emotional body. If your parents had these judgments, then you inherited them. The process began with your conception. When your father had sex with your mother the energy of his orgasm influenced, or colored, your earliest perceptions. As a fetus, you were the same organism as your mother and it was therefore not possible for you to be unaffected by her emotional repression. Your parents had to survive their own developmental processes. To survive those processes and gain acceptance from our parents, most of us have to violate our instincts and suppress our emotions. We learn very quickly that love and acceptance are given to those who embrace stuffing their emotions. The judgment, "Don't feel and don't emote," is reinforced again and again as we grow older and is usually passed from one generation to another.

112

Guilt. If your emotions are allowed to emote in an appropriate way at the time they are experienced, your organism will energetically return to a place of balance and understanding. Violating this process produces feelings of guilt because we have violated the natural process of the natural order.

Atonement. Atonement is an attempt to move out of guilt in order to reconnect with the repressed emotions. Because you learned that emotions are not acceptable, you had to find new and creative ways to release them, except now your emotions have been stuffed into a state of unconsciousness. Since a functional/conscious release is unavailable, you try to move the emotions in unconscious ways. You might, for example, move them unconsciously in caretaking and enabling behaviors. Caretakers perform basic life functions for others and, in the process, deprive others of taking responsibility for their own lives. Mothers, for example, often become caretakers when they do all the cooking and cleaning for their adolescent children rather than teaching them how to do these things for themselves. Your governments often function in the same way. Enablers make excuses for others' dysfunctional behaviors and support them in their continuing avoidance of their core issues. Eventually caretakers, enablers, and others who love to atone will experience themselves as victims and declare how they are suffering.

Suffering. When you create enough suffering you will create new emotions, usually grief and anger. But these emotions are usually denied also, so the cycle begins again.

Unconsciously, people enter into relationships for the purpose of healing their spirit by creating opportunities to move their repressed emotions. It is through your emotional body that experiences are drawn to you. Karma is an attempt to heal emotions that have become unconscious essence. Usually you will not know in advance when you are being drawn into a karmically based abusive situation, because the emotional essence drawing you into the experience is unconscious.

For attraction to take place there must be feelings of familiarity present. The ego justifies feelings of familiarity with such external observations as: attractiveness, liking the same kinds of music, similar experiences in life, etc. In reality, the original cause or unresolved emotional issue from this or previous lives is the ultimate basis for the attraction. The term "like attracts like," means that you and your partner are functioning at similar levels of awareness and are together in order to trigger the release of your repressed emotions and reintegrate your fragmented essence. Battered women stay in their abusive relationships until they are willing to deal with their repressed anger. The more a woman continues to deny the emotions being triggered when she is being abused, the more guilt she is embracing. People remain in abusive relationships because they are in denial of their personal power. This denied personal power creates guilt, and guilt creates the need for atonement. Often, in an abusive relationship one person is addicted to atonement, while the other is addicted to releasing anger in dysfunctional ways.

114

As an individual you have emotional, mental, spiritual, and physical aspects. You can be focused on any one of these aspects at any time during your life. Likewise, you can be in denial and deny the emotional, mental, spiritual, or physical. If you do, you will feel guilt, which begets atonement, which begets suffering, which begets emotions, etc. You know the rest of this story by now. If you want to come out of your darkness and into your truth, just deal with your denials. The truth is so very simple.

Most of you—if you are honest—will be able to admit that your lives are a reflection of all the things you don't want. Most of you are existing without experiencing who you really are. You have become so rigid and frozen in your illusionary beliefs that you can't imagine how life could be any other way.

I AM telling you that it can be different. You can live your dreams. But you must learn to be honest with yourself and with those with whom you interact. The greatest obstacle in your life is you. You fear that if you have everything you desire, it will all be taken away. And you doubt that you can have everything in your life because you doubt that you are worthy to receive all you desire. Life is abundant, and there is enough abundance on this planet for all. Some of you are not only unwilling to share, but you have hoarded others' shares. If you remember back to the early days of your childhood, you will remember that you did not tolerate greed. Back then you were not afraid to move your emotions when you felt like you were being taken. What happened to you that caused you to abandon your truth? Now you do little or nothing about the injustice all life is receiving. You violated your Will when you decided to be a grown-up and play with the grown-ups. To play with the grown-ups you must play by their rules, and their rules are: denial, guilt, atonement, suffering, and the stuffing or dysfunctional movement of emotion.

There is a difference between acting childish, and being childlike. A child is real with her/his feelings, whereas childish behavior indicates the denial of feelings. In order to escape the dysfunctional cycle in which you imprison yourself, you will have to become as a child. You will have to relearn that it is okay to be yourself, to cry when you are feeling pain, for example, and that it's similarly okay to be angry, scared, etc. If you cannot learn to accept yourself— which means loving yourself—then you will never be free from the destructive behaviors which surround your highest truth. You will never be free from the karmic wheel of life.

CHAPTER XII

Forgiveness and Healing

Heaven on earth can only become a reality when forgiveness of self and others is achieved. Initially, you may
find it difficult to forgive those who have violated you.
Know that those who deserve to be punished, will be punished. Mother–Father God is a very merciful presence and
you need to trust that everyone draws to themselves a reflection of the denials of their chosen path.

I AM asking you to make peace with yourself by dealing with your emotions. Your organism is designed to push
up and release anything that is unlike love. If you accept

and encourage this process by moving your emotions in a functional way you will eventually discover the love that is within you. If you are in a state of love, forgiveness will automatically emerge. The individual I have chosen to deliver this book has suffered greatly from physical abuse in this life. The abuse received from her/his biological mother has caused this individual to feel considerable grief, anger and terror. By going into these emotions and experiencing their full fury, this individual was able to release their charge. In so doing she/he discovered that her/his biological mother does not hate her/him. Ultimately, as a result of this process, she/he discovered the presence of Mother–Father God within her/himself.

Let me state this again in a slightly different way, just to be sure you understand it. If you are filled with repressed emotions, remove your focus from the external person or circumstances that stimulated the emotions and instead focus on how you can release your emotions in a way that will not violate another. If you do this you will eventually discover the love that is within you.

The human ego creates great resistance to change. The function of the ego is to relate experiences to practical everyday living and to evolve with Spirit through these experiences. Without ego's presence, there would be no sense of self. Ego is your ability to "embrace" or to "release" judgments. There are not "good" feelings and "bad" feelings, just many judgments against certain feelings. Embracing these judgments prevents you from knowing the truth. There are as many ways for ego to define what love is and what love is not as there are grains of sand on a beach. What one ego defines as heaven might be how another ego defines hell. What leads an individual into wholeness is a sacred story in which the ego is both the author and the actress/actor. You are each your own judge, juror, executioner and "savior."

Prepare your ego for the real purpose of your presence on this earth—to know and to remember that you are the manifestation of Mother–Father God. That which you serve is that which you are. That which you long to become is that which you already are. Stand in your power and in so doing reflect truth to those who have as yet been unwilling to open their ears and their eyes and their hearts to the wisdom that you have chosen to hear. The body of Christ is made up of many cells. You are one of those cells. Your body of work is to follow your Heart, and in so doing, teach others how to follow their Hearts. How you choose to do this is of your own choosing. You always have free Will choice. You are exactly where you need to be. With depth of feeling you may ask to be led into your highest truth. We will hear your prayers. As a fire fighter is compelled to answer the call to put out a fire, so too is Mother–Father God compelled to manifest your desires to heal and to become as One.

You do not willingly embrace your flesh body because of all the repressed emotions that are being held in the body. These repressed emotions have voices that can be heard through the internal fragments of you. They can easily be heard if you will turn inward and listen. It is very important to let them speak because they have so much to teach you. It should not surprise you that divisive energy has instructed mental health professionals to label you as crazy if you are hearing voices. It does this because it does not want people to become conscious of the fact that what they are really hearing is the voice of their own fragmented essence. The truth is, you already know how to be whole. I AM hoping that this book will help to remind you.

The voice of your Mighty I AM presence never speaks with duality. Rather, it is the voice in the silence that speaks when you are quietly receptive. You have been given two ears and two eyes and one mouth. Hear and see twice as much as you speak. You need to meditate to hear your truth. In meditation, if you have commanded in the name of the Christ/Heart to hear the highest truth, know that you will. Be willing to question that which you hear. Do not settle for just one answer; rather, be willing to probe for deeper understandings by asking, "Why is this so?" Let each question find an answer, and let each answer lead you to another question. I AM asking you to make Spirit work harder for you. Know that I AM without limit. The connection most of you have with your Spirit is like a physical body that has been bedridden for a very long time. Your spiritual muscles have become very weak. The presence of Spirit needs to be exercised in order to function with optimum efficiency. Spirit feels equally awkward in communicating with the ego as the ego does with Spirit. The only way to bridge this gap is through desire, and you are not without desire.

120

Do not attempt to dominate your feelings/emotions. Instead, be with them; in so doing, you will evolve them. Be as a child who screams when in fear, cries when in pain, and laughs when in joy. Be with your fear of the darkness for it is only in the darkness that you will recognize yourself as light/life/love. Beloved, if you will take one step, I will take two.

One method I suggest using to get in touch with your feelings is re-birthing. Re-birthing is nothing more than allowing yourself to re-experience old traumas from this life as well as from others. It is being born again to the lost remembrances of past experiences. Some call this soul retrieval. It is very helpful to find someone whom you trust who can facilitate this experience. There are those who have volunteered for this service. There are many references in the Bible about being born again. **"No one shall see the Kingdom of Mother–Father God unless they be born again."** When you have a re-birth experience, you again experience yourself reliving the thoughts and feelings that originated at birth or during some other traumatic experience. You can go as far back into your history this way as is necessary. **"You cannot look upon the face of Mother–Father God and live,"** because once you have experienced yourself as an immortal Spirit, your perceptions of who you think you are fall away. What replaces them is the truth, and you can no longer continue to live your life in the same ways. Symbolically, your false self dies. This is how you are born again.

The greatest gift you can give yourself is to be unconditionally loving of your Self—for you are the embodiment and manifestation of Mother–Father God. The second greatest gift is to be able to dialogue with the spiritual essence within you and to hear and accept the truths that are offered to you.

You are misled when you give away your power to "experts" and institutions outside yourselves that profess to know the "truth." If these "experts" and institutions are preaching, alleging, advertising, etc., etc., that they know the truth and you don't, then they are attempting to seduce you into the illusionary belief that you are separate from Mother–Father God and that only through an intermediary—namely them—can this split be healed. This is an illusionary belief if ever there was one. There is only Oneness, and anything that appears otherwise is an illusion.

Remember that thoughts/illusions are as clouds floating across the sky. Some clouds—like your thoughts/illusions—are dark and stormy; others are bright and beautiful. You are like the sky, and the thoughts/illusions are but passing clouds. You are eternal, as is the wisdom of Heart. Illusionary thoughts originating in ego will—in time— evaporate, just as the density of ice turns to water and water turns to steam as its molecular vibration increases.

When you turn inward to listen to the voice of Heart, you must listen with discrimination for you will also hear many discordant voices. These voices have been lost to love's light, and are as lost children in need of the loving parenting they never received. They are likely to bombard you with false/disruptive thoughts. These disruptive thoughts will linger to the degree to which you have abandoned your emotional body. That could be a few months or many years. You must learn to embrace it all, and to give acceptance for whatever is being said. If very angry voices are speaking destructive thoughts, encouraging you to harm yourself or others, it will be necessary to move this charge of hatred in a functional way. As you become more responsive to the needs of your emotional body and begin to release the charges of repressed emotional energy that are blocked, you will begin to experience more love, joy, and, ultimately, "the peace that passes all understanding."

As your emotional body moves its repressed charge, you will hear the voice of Heart. In time Heart's voice will be joined by the voices of Will, Spirit, and Form. You need to become receptive/sensitive to the needs of all aspects of your being. Your Will needs to be allowed to move emotionally. Your Spirit needs to be given acceptance as the guiding intelligence in your life. Your Heart needs to be allowed to balance and integrate with all aspects of Form. Finally, your Form/physical identity needs to be allowed to have a healthy and abundant existence.

You have many different personalities within: the lost child, the protector, the saint, the good, the bad, and the ugly, etc. One effective technique for contacting the different voices inside yourself is to sit and write whatever comes to mind. Do this for several hours or for as long as you can.

Another way is to write with your non-dominant hand. You will be surprised at what will be said.

Your body is going to re-experience the traumas of held emotional energy. When this energy begins to rise into consciousness for the purpose of release and healing, stress will be created in your body. Epsom salt baths can be very helpful in allowing your muscles to release stress-induced contractions. When the charge of emotion again becomes active in the muscle tissue it can sometimes pull the skeletal structure out of place. It may be necessary to seek out the services of an osteopath, body worker, or a chiropractor.

All illness can be linked to emotional/spiritual denial. Modern medicine does not deal with the cause of illness but rather with the effect of illness. If people accepted their Hearts, open-heart surgery and heart attacks would not be necessary. They would never allow themselves to digest the animal fats which plug up the arteries. There are many references in the Bible in Leviticus concerning the avoidance of animal fat in one's diet. To become a physician you must spend all your time being in your head, studying your textbooks. This prevents you from being with your body and all that the body is. It is difficult for disease to manifest in a body which has been sustained with high levels of oxygen, a healthy diet, and a manifest desire to heal the emotional/spiritual imbalances that you have incarnated on earth to heal.

Healing will involve consciously guided deep breathing techniques and body work which is going to trigger emotions, the release of which is going to facilitate healing. As it is now, physicians prescribe consciousness altering substances designed to numb one from her/his emotional awareness. Medicine, as it is practiced today, will someday be viewed as barbaric. As long as the body is seen as only a physical vehicle, instead of Mother–Father God's light, the body will be violated with knives cutting away those parts of the Will that are so denied that their only choice is to fragment out of the body. I AM not suggesting that you avoid surgery if it can prolong your life. What I AM suggesting is that you learn to view illness and dis-ease as a means of recognizing that there is emotional essence/Will that is not being embraced. Use your illness as a means to connect more deeply with your Form/Will by being as present with your symptoms as you possibly can, and feeling the underlying emotions.

The more quickly you can move through your rage, your grief, your terror, your shame etc., the more quickly you will heal. Move your rage with a physical expression that is safe for you and others. Move your rage until you can feel that your rage is really loving essence that has been blocked in its natural attempt to recover from being made powerless. You will find that rage and terror, as well as grief and terror, often cover one another. Know that your I AM presence will not give you more than you can handle at any one time. As you progress into deeper levels of emotional movement, you may need a partner or partners to make the movement of these deeper feelings safe to release. I urge you to be

125

creative, but do not inflict harm. When working with another, always agree on a code word such as "stop," that will indicate that you have had enough. Yelling, screaming, moaning, groaning, etc. are essential for the release of your emotions. The reason the charge is there to begin with is because, originally, you failed to speak up for yourself. Now you are an adult and you do have a voice. Use it.

Do not beat yourself up if you are having problems with your addictions or other destructive behaviors. You will find that as you clear your emotional charge, your body will return to a higher vibration. Eventually you will have no need for your addictions because, if you are vibrating at a higher frequency, your addictions will become repulsive to you.

Ego is going to create resistance to emotional movement. If there is resistance, beginning to move rage while yelling "I won't, you can't make me," is often enough to connect with the rage beneath the resistance. Each time you move emotionally, you will be integrating a lost fragment of yourself. Eventually you will look forward to this, because of the feelings of joy and wholeness you will experience at the moment of integration.

It is very important that you move your rage, terror and grief toward me and toward Mother–Father God. We will not abandon you, nor will we judge your movement as unloving. It is, in fact, the repressed charges of energy that you are holding that prevent us from being in your life. We understand and accept the emotional movement

126

that is necessary for your healing. The more emotion you move, the more our presence will become a reality in your life.

The feelings, thoughts, illusions, and beliefs that you choose to embrace as truth will become your reality. I AM asking you to embrace the truth that you are not separate from Mother–Father God's Heart. I AM asking you to call into your body/life, with your free Will choice, their presence so as to intensify the reality of their existence in your life. Nothing can exist without the presence of our love. I AM asking you to declare out loud your intent to heal. When there is intent/desire to heal, healing will manifest. Whatever you focus your thoughts and feelings on is the reality you create. I AM asking you to focus your thoughts and feelings on the truth that you are a manifestation of Mother–Father God's love/Heart, and in so doing become the only begotten daughter/son of Mother–Father God.

CHAPTER XIII

Fulfillment

Fulfillment—or self-realization—is not something you stumble upon one day, never to again know discontentment. Fulfillment is something you create; it is an evolving state of being without limit. The emotional body incorporates all emotions and is immortal. Therefore, there is no permanent state that is without pain. Mother–Father God created all things, knows all things, and feels all things. Fulfillment, or the peace that surpasses all understanding, is born in the Heart of Mother–Father God—the very Heart manifest within you that eternally awaits your acceptance. **"Know the truth and the truth shall make you free."**

You are the creator of your own desires; you are the only one capable of fulfilling your desires; and you are the only one capable of blocking the fulfillment of your desires. You are the only one who knows which patterns of behavior are no longer useful; and you are the only one capable of making these changes. Only you can claim your identity and, as you do, you will find deeper levels of fulfillment.

YOU WILL NOT FIND ME UNTIL YOU FIND ME WITHIN YOURSELF. The more you release your emotions, the more deeply you will understand the truth about yourself and others. In accepting and allowing expression in your emotional body, you will create space within the physical body to receive the abundance of love and joy that is your birthright and heritage. Understanding and acceptance enable you to view discordant issues from a place of power. Heal your emotional body and you will remove the resistance that prevents you from knowing the fullness of Mother–Father God's love. You were born to claim the love, the power, and the wisdom, that is rightfully yours. You were born to be free; now is the time to claim that freedom. **"My time has not yet come, but your time is always ready. The world cannot hate you, but it hates Me because I testify of it that its works are evil."**

Jesus answered then, "Many good works I have shown you from my Mother–Father God. For which of these works do you stone me? The Jews answered him, saying, "For a good work we do not stone you, but for blasphemy, and because you being a man, make yourself God." Jesus answered them, "Is it not written in your law, you are gods?"

AMEN

JESUS, THE CHRISTED